The Eat Raw KITCHEN

The
Eat Raw
KITCHEN

*Feel-good food for
happy and healthy eating*

This edition published by Parragon Books Ltd in 2016
LOVE FOOD is an imprint of Parragon Books Ltd

Parragon Books Ltd
Chartist House
15–17 Trim Street
Bath BA1 1HA, UK
www.parragon.com/lovefood

ISBN 978-1-4748-3796-5

Printed in China

New recipes and introduction by Judith Wills
Cover photography by Tony Briscoe
New recipe photography by Al Richardson and
home economy and food styling by Laurie Perry

NOTES FOR THE READER

This book uses both metric and imperial measurements. Follow
the same units of measurement throughout; do not mix metric
and imperial. All spoon measurements are level: teaspoons
are assumed to be 5 ml, and tablespoons are assumed to be
15 ml. Unless otherwise stated, milk is assumed to be full fat,
eggs and individual fruits and vegetables are medium, pepper
is freshly ground black pepper and salt is table salt. A pinch
of salt is calculated as $1/16$ of a teaspoon. Unless otherwise
stated, all root vegetables should be peeled prior to using.

Any recipes using sprouting seeds, sometimes called salad
sprouts, should be avoided by children younger than five,
older adults, pregnant women and those with weakened
immune systems, who are particularly vulnerable to the
bacteria that may be present on sprouts.

The times given are an approximate guide only. Preparation
times will differ according to the techniques used by
different people. Please note that any ingredients stated
as being optional are not included in the nutritional values
provided. The nutritional values given are approximate
and provided as a guideline only, they do not account for
individual cooks, scales and portion sizes. The nutritional
values provided are per serving or per item.

CONTENTS

WHY RAW FOOD?

As more and more of us across the world realize that true health comes from choosing a natural lifestyle and diet, there has been a significant increase in the number of people looking for a perfect, healthy, clean and environmentally sound way to eat. For hundreds of thousands of us, this diet is summed up by two words: eating raw.

Eating raw food can best be described as a philosophy or a set of choices rather than a set of rules. That said, most raw food eaters will agree that the diet consists of fresh, wholesome food that has not been cooked above a temperature of 40°C/104°F, has not been highly processed, has not had important elements removed, and has not been adulterated with unnatural additives.

Such a diet usually simply consists of vegetables, fruits, seeds, nuts, sprouts and plant oils. While some people following a raw food diet will also eat raw meat, fish, dairy produce and eggs, the recipes in this book are based on plant foods alone and are therefore suitable for a vegan diet.

WHO MAY BENEFIT FROM EATING RAW?
There are many potential health benefits in eating a raw food diet. Raw foodists, as they are sometimes termed, frequently say they have noticed several of the following advantages after just a few weeks of raw eating: improved digestion, improved immunity to problems such as colds and eczema, reduction in fluid retention and bloating, an end to food cravings, increased mental and physical energy, better skin, and an improved mood.

The raw food diet is believed to help reverse type 2 diabetes or prevent the condition developing. It is also a very natural and simple way to lose weight, and long term may offer protection against the diseases of ageing, such as cardio-vascular disease, cancers, and arthritis. This may be because of the high levels of antioxidant plant compounds in the diet, the preservation of nutrients destroyed by cooking, as well as its avoidance of so-called 'junk foods'.

Eating raw can also help conserve our world by reducing the amount of energy we consume, and is perhaps the ideal way to eat for those concerned with food sustainability and environmental impact. Many raw food eaters also prefer to choose organic and in-season foods.

YOUR CHOICE
Whether you choose to eat 50%, 75% or 100% raw, including healthy raw foods and meals more often in your diet is a positive choice and one you will not regret.

SO WHAT IS A RAW FOOD DIET?

The raw vegan diet is typically made up of 75% fruits and vegetables in addition to seaweed, sprouted seeds, grains and pulses, dried fruits, and nuts. The recipes that follow demonstrate just how versatile this selection of foods can be.

RAW FOOD STAPLES
• Fruits, such as oranges, bananas, raspberries, blueberries and avocado
• Fresh vegetables, such as carrots, parsnips, beans and cucumber
• Leafy greens, including kale, spinach, broccoli, cabbage and lettuce
• Soaked raw nuts and seeds
• Sprouted grains, such as quinoa, millet and buckwheat
• Sprouted legumes, including lentils, chickpeas and beans
• Probiotic-rich foods such as raw yogurt and raw sauerkraut

FOODS TO WATCH OUT FOR
Frozen fruit and vegetables are raw as long as they haven't been steamed or boiled to blanch before freezing, so it's best to avoid packaged frozen fruit and vegetables.

Canned foods, such as pulses or vegetables, are not raw as the canning process uses high heat.

Pasteurized foods are not raw due to the process involved. In the USA, this includes most almonds which are pasteurized by law. Exceptions include raw almonds sold direct to the public by almond growers, and imported raw almonds.

Dried herbs and spices – some of these, such as black pepper, and spices such as cloves, cumin and nutmeg are considered raw.

Condiments – soy sauce and most bottled condiments are not raw, but some raw foodists eat these in moderation. Alternatives are nama shoyu, an unpasteurized soy sauce – not technically raw as it is still heated – or raw coconut aminos, made from coconut sap and aged naturally.

Sugar substitutes – a good raw option is Medjool dates which can be soaked and pureed, raw agave nectars, stevia and coconut palm sugar. Maple syrup is also used – not raw but some brands are less processed than others. Raw honey is fine (although not vegan) and can be used in place of agave nectar or maple syrup.

Salt – raw salts include sun-dried sea salt and Himalayan pink salt. Standard table salt is not raw.

WHAT CAN I DRINK?
Many who follow a raw food diet like to avoid the impurities present in tap water and even filtered water, and prefer alkalized water or ionized water. Use what you feel comfortable with.

Smoothies and juices made from raw ingredients are fine and nutritious.

Tea and coffee are often avoided because the leaves/beans are processed using heat. Home-picked herbal teas are an excellent alternative.

Alcohol is avoided, but wine is considered a raw item – organic wines contain fewer sulphites.

STARTING A RAW DIET

Any increase in the amount of raw food you eat is likely to benefit your health. If you want to adopt a strict raw diet, it is probably wise to make a gradual transition to raw food. So if you are vegan, for example, you could increase the amount of raw food you eat by a little each week.

Similarly, if you are currently following a standard diet incorporating cooked meat, fish and eggs, start the transition to raw food slowly, gradually increasing your intake of vegetables, fruit and nuts by replacing animal products. If during this time you get any discomfort in your digestive tract or bowels, take things more slowly.

You can also choose a long-term high raw diet but still include some non-raw items, either as a vegan, vegetarian or, if you prefer, still eating a little fish, dairy or even meat. Many choose to do this, and any increase in raw food is likely to have associated benefits.

These ideas will help you avoid any 'detox' symptoms such as headaches or stomach upsets which can occur if you change your diet too quickly, as well as minimizing the chance of getting cravings for sweet, salty or 'junk' foods. Any cravings should disappear within two weeks.

GETTING ENOUGH NUTRIENTS

A typical well-balanced raw food vegan diet will contain virtually all the vitamins, minerals and other nutrients that you need for good health. You can ensure a good balance by doing the following:

* Eating to provide your body with enough calories. Raw vegan eating is an excellent way to lose weight because many plant foods provide bulk for few calories because of their high water content. But you need to eat sufficient to give your body the energy and nutrients it needs. Include enough of the high-calorie items such as nuts, seeds, fruits naturally high in sugar (e.g. dates and bananas) and root vegetables to provide the calories you need daily (around 2500 for adult males and 2000 for females). If you're very active you may need more.

* Eating a wide range of foods. The raw vegan diet avoids all animal products and so it is important to get a wide range of other foods every day.

An easy way to get a good variety of vitamins, plant chemicals and minerals is to have several different colours on your plate at each meal (dark green, orange, red and purple for example), while a range of types of food (leaves, fruits, seeds, nuts and pulses, for example) should ensure you get enough of the amino acids that make up complete protein, as well as adequate carbohydrate, fat and minerals.

RAW FOOD EQUIPMENT

Because raw food is not cooked, the emphasis is always on the preparation of ingredients. While there are some pieces of equipment that will make your life easier if you plan to focus on a raw food diet, all you need is a selection of sharp knives and an electric blender.

A range of good knives could include a 20 cm/8 inch sharp cook's knife for chopping vegetables and fruit, a serrated knife with a blunt end with a 12–cm/5–inch blade for slicing; and a similar small straight–edge knife for peeling vegetables and fruit. An electric blender is indispensable for making smoothies, blended soups and purées. A processor will also make light work of chopping, grinding and nut butters.

Useful, but not essential, is a dehydrator. This is a small electric 'oven' with racks and trays inside, usually with two heat settings, high (60°C/140°F) and low (45°C/115°F) so that you can dry foods such as biscuits, breads and fruits without cooking them. This will increase the texture and variety of the food you prepare.

If you don't want to buy a dehydrator, many electric cookers have at least one setting low enough to dehydrate foods at the right heat. This may be the defrost setting or a designated dehydrate setting. To check the temperature of your oven on these settings, you can purchase an inexpensive oven thermometer. A standard oven, unless it has a dehydrate setting, won't be able to dehydrate in the same way as a dehydrator, so using an oven may mean that what you are preparing may not be 100% raw.

A juicer is invaluable so you can juice fruits and vegetables, a method which removes the insoluble fibre allowing you to better absorb the nutrients in the fruit and vegetables. The best juicer for preserving the nutrients is a masticating (slow) juicer. Smoothies are also a popular choice – these retain all the goodness and fibre of the contents, but slow down digestion, therefore keeping you full for longer. Because oxidization occurs with blending, which undermines the nutritional value of the contents, shorter blending times are advisable. It's best to do the bulk of your blending on a low speed, which doesn't create much oxidation, and limit the amount of time blending on a high speed.

Handheld and stand mandolines are useful for slicing fruit and vegetables quickly and efficiently. Interchangeable blades mean you can also dice, make 'fries' and so on. A spiralizer can be used for making 'spaghetti' using vegetables such as courgettes and squash.

It is important to practise good kitchen hygiene to avoid contact with harmful bacteria and moulds – so wash your hands before preparing foods, eat foods as fresh as you can and store them in cool conditions. If you share a kitchen with people who eat animal produce, keep separate chopping boards and utensils for yourself to avoid contamination.

RAW FOOD PREPARATION

NUT SOAKING

Many raw eaters prefer to soak nuts to make them more easily digested, activate the beneficial enzymes and increase the availability of the nutrients. Soaked nuts can also be processed more quickly to make butters and dips. Nuts are usually soaked for 8–12 hours. After soaking and draining, you can dehydrate them (12 hours or more will be necessary) and store as for unsoaked nuts.

NUT BUTTERS

Recipes in this book requiring nut butters include methods for making them in the recipe, but ready-made raw versions can be easily sourced – just make sure the label states raw and sugar-free.

SPROUTING

You can sprout your own seeds, pulses, grains and nuts either by using the jar or the tray method. In each case, soak the seeds overnight in water, then drain. Wash sprouted foods well before eating and consume them soon after harvesting.

For the jar method, add seeds to a sealed jar with 1–2 tbsp water and cover the top of the jar with muslin before putting an outer lid over the cloth. Invert the jar over a tray and leave it slightly tilted (propped against the wall of the tray) so air can get into the jar. Leave at room temperature and drain and rinse twice a day until the seeds sprout.

For the tray method, you can buy a variety of single or multi-tiered sprouting trays or simply use a seed tray lined with sturdy kitchen paper. Keep the paper wet and rinse and drain the seeds twice a day until they sprout.

RAW COCONUT YOGURT

Raw coconut yogurt is a great addition to the raw food diet. You can also buy raw coconut yogurt ready made. Coconut yogurt is featured in a number of the recipes in this book. This method will produce a medium-thick yogurt – you can adjust the amount of coconut water to make yogurt of a thickness to your own liking. This makes around 600 ml/1 pint, or 4 servings.

Ingredients

150 ml/5 fl oz raw coconut water
450 g/1 lb raw white coconut meat,
    roughly chopped
2 probiotic powder capsules, found in health-food
    stores/online

Method

1. Process the coconut meat with a little of the coconut water until it is thoroughly blended and then add the rest of the water and blend again until smooth.

2. Break open the probiotic capsules and sprinkle the powder contents into the blender; pulse for a few seconds.

3. Pour the mixture into a large wide necked jar. Put the lid on and leave the jar in a warm kitchen or room for up to 16 hours until you have a yogurt mixture. Flavour as liked. You can store the yogurt in the fridge for several days.

F.A.Q. ABOUT RAW FOOD

WHY ARE UNCOOKED FOODS BEST?

Raw food eaters believe that cooking food destroys much of its nutrients including vitamins, minerals, enzymes and plant chemicals. They also believe that raw food is more easily digested and absorbed by the body.

WILL I GET ENOUGH NUTRIENTS?

People on a vegan raw food diet may have a shortfall on calcium, iron and vitamin B12. The best raw sources of calcium include nuts, seeds and leafy greens. Good sources of iron in a raw diet include pulses, nori seaweed, nuts and seeds, dark leafy greens, and dried apricots. Vitamin B12 is hard to get on a vegan diet, but the best source is dried nori seaweed, around 4 g/$\frac{1}{8}$ oz would give a daily supply, and shiitake mushrooms is a good source too. Vitamin B12 supplements are easily available.

A raw food diet that includes animal and/or dairy produce is unlikely to provide any deficiencies.

WHERE WILL I GET MY PROTEIN?

Pulses such as lentils and chickpeas as well as hemp seeds and quinoa are good sources of protein and all can be eaten raw when sprouted. Fresh legumes such as peas and edamame beans are useful sources, while a wide range of vegetables contain protein in differing amounts. As long as you get a variety and sufficiency of protein-containing foods every day you will not go short of any necessary amino acids.

WILL I NEED TO TAKE SUPPLEMENTS?

If you have an adequate and varied diet, there should be no need to take supplements, with the possible exception of vitamin B12 (see column to left).

WILL PREPARING FOOD TAKE AGES?

You can spend as little or as much time on food preparation as you like. Raw salads, smoothies and soups are quick to prepare. Some dishes require more chopping, processing and preparation but a processor and blender, and perhaps a mandolin slicer, save time. Cooking time is nil – and if you use a dehydrator this needs little tending while food is dried. 'Plan ahead' is the best tip.

SHOULD I USE ORGANIC FRUITS AND VEGETABLES?

Many raw food eaters prefer to eat organically so they know they are eating only natural, unprocessed foods. The flavour and nutrient content of raw plant foods may be superior to non-organic.

WILL I EXPERIENCE PHYSICAL SYMPTOMS?

Introduce yourself to raw eating gradually and you should not experience adverse symptoms. Your bowels may become more regular due to the additional fibre and water in your diet. Initially you may get a headache, especially if you are withdrawing from caffeine-rich drinks. Most people report a range of positive improvements in how they feel a few weeks into their raw diet – including more energy, improvements in digestion, better skin and better sleep.

BREAKFASTS

Blueberry porridge pie	20
Acai and berry morning jar	22
Buckwheat breakfast bowl	24
Pear, banana and apple breakfast bowl	26
Very berry overnight oats	28
Buckwheat granola bars	30
Natural blackberry bars	32
Wake-up salad	34
Beetroot and pomegranate smoothie bowl	36
Morning power bowl smoothie	38
Matcha power smoothie	40
Power gulp	42

BLUEBERRY PORRIDGE PIE

Here's a delicious, fibre-rich porridge packed with fruit and topped with a sweet, sticky and crunchy crumble. Everyone will love this!

SERVES: 2
PREP: 15 MINS, PLUS SOAKING

85 g/3 oz raw rolled oats
1½ tsp chia seeds
2½ tbsp raw dried coconut flakes
¾ tsp ground cinnamon
1 banana, peeled and roughly chopped
juice of ¼ lemon
1¾ tbsp raw honey
60 g/2¼ oz blueberries
225 ml/8 fl oz raw coconut milk
2 tbsp chopped raw almonds
½ tbsp milled flaxseed
1 tbsp sunflower seeds

1. Combine the oats, chia seeds, 2 tablespoons of the coconut flakes and half a teaspoon of the cinnamon in a mixing bowl.

2. Put the banana pieces in a small bowl. Sprinkle over the lemon juice and stir in 1 tablespoon of the honey, making sure each piece of banana is coated with the mixture. (You can warm the honey slightly if it's too solid to stir in.)

3. Stir the bananas, half the blueberries and the coconut milk into the oat mixture and combine. Spoon evenly into two serving bowls, pressing the banana pieces into the porridge. Cover the bowls with clingfilm or foil and leave in the fridge overnight.

4. Meanwhile, start making the pie topping. In a small bowl, stir the almonds, flaxseed and sunflower seeds together. Stir in the remaining cinnamon and honey, warmed if necessary. Mix thoroughly and leave covered for the morning.

5. Before serving, sprinkle the topping over the porridge and decorate with the remaining coconut flakes and blueberries.

WARM PORRIDGE
While the porridge tastes great served cold, it can also be warmed gently to 40°C/104°F before you add the topping.

PER SERVING: 582 KCALS | 29.6G FAT | 17.1G SAT FAT | 75G CARBS | 29.4G SUGARS | 14.6G FIBRE | 12G PROTEIN | TRACE SALT

ACAI AND BERRY MORNING JAR

*This breakfast jar is pretty to look at and quick to make.
After chilling it in the fridge overnight, all you need to do is pop
the topping on for breakfast – or, indeed, any meal of the day!*

SERVES: 1
PREP: 10 MINS, PLUS RESTING AND CHILLING

90 g/3¼ oz strawberries
90 g/3¼ oz raspberries
35 g/1¼ oz blueberries
150 g/5½ oz raw coconut yogurt (see recipe below)
50 ml/2 fl oz raw coconut milk
½ tsp seeds from 1 vanilla pod
1 tbsp chia seeds
2 tsp raw honey
1 tsp acai powder
½ tbsp lemon juice
2 tbsp raw cashew butter
1 tsp hemp seeds
2 fresh mint sprigs

RAW COCONUT YOGURT

225 g/8 oz fresh or frozen coconut meat,
thawed if frozen
100 ml/3½ fl oz raw coconut water
1 probiotic powder capsule

1. To make the coconut yogurt, blend the coconut meat and coconut water in a blender until smooth. Empty the powder from the probiotic capsule into the mixture and blend again for a few seconds.

2. Pour the coconut mixture into a bowl, cover with clingfilm or foil, and leave in the kitchen overnight at warm room temperature. In the morning, you should have about 300 g/10½ oz yogurt. Remove what you need and the rest will keep in the fridge for up to a week.

3. Blend 75 g/2½ oz strawberries, 75 g/2½ oz raspberries and 30 g/1 oz blueberries with the yogurt, coconut milk, vanilla seeds, chia seeds, honey, acai powder and lemon juice until smooth. Pour the mixture into a wide-necked jar with a 300–325 ml/10–11 fl oz capacity. Cover and chill in the fridge overnight.

4. The following morning, top with the cashew butter and the remaining berries, followed by the hemp seeds and mint sprigs.

CHIA CHARM
Chia seeds can be used to thicken smoothies and desserts. They also provide essential vitamins, minerals and omega-3 fats.

PER SERVING: 897 KCALS | 67.3G FAT | 42.7G SAT FAT | 72.1G CARBS | 34.6G SUGARS | 26.9G FIBRE | 15.4G PROTEIN | 0.1G SALT

BUCKWHEAT BREAKFAST BOWL

Buckwheat has been eaten since Paleolithic times. It makes a tasty cereal and, being a source of complex carbohydrates, provides an excellent boost of energy.

SERVES: 4
PREP: 20–25 MINS, PLUS 36 HRS SPROUTING

150 g/5½ oz buckwheat
500 ml/18 fl oz cold water
400 g/14 oz coconut yogurt
grated zest and juice of 1 orange
3 tbsp goji berries
100 g/3½ oz raspberries
1 Granny Smith apple, cored and diced
1 tbsp pumpkin seeds
2 passion fruit, pulp only
2 tsp ground cinnamon
½ tsp ground turmeric
seeds of 1 pomegranate
2 tbsp agave syrup

1. Rinse the buckwheat three times in fresh water to clean the groats. Place in a bowl with the cold water. Soak for 30 minutes.

2. Drain and rinse the buckwheat, and leave at room temperature – in either a sprouting tray or a sieve with a bowl beneath – for 36 hours. Rinse the buckwheat if the groats look sticky, and then once more before using.

3. Rinse, drain and divide the buckwheat between four bowls. Divide the yogurt, sprinkle over the remaining ingredients and serve.

SPROUTING SECRETS

This recipe uses buckwheat that has been sprouted for 36 hours; it can be done in less, but a longer time gives optimum nutrition.

Note: recipes using sprouting seeds should be avoided by children younger than five, older adults, pregnant women and those with weakened immune systems, who are particularly vulnerable to the bacteria that may be present on sprouts.

PER SERVING: 452 KCALS | 22.4G FAT | 17.5G SAT FAT | 58G CARBS | 22.8G SUGARS | 9.8G FIBRE | 10.1G PROTEIN | 0.1G SALT

PEAR, BANANA AND APPLE BREAKFAST BOWL

If you're tired of eating grains for breakfast, this fruity breakfast bowl will invigorate — it's full of fresh autumnal flavours, fiery cinnamon and delicious dried berries.

SERVES: 2
PREP: 10 MINS, PLUS OPTIONAL CHILLING

2 ripe dessert pears
2 green-skinned apples, such as Granny Smith
1 large banana, peeled and chopped
75 ml/2½ fl oz apple juice
juice of ½ lemon
2 tbsp sultanas
2 tbsp raw cashew nuts
1 tbsp sunflower seeds
1 tbsp raw sugar
½ tsp ground cinnamon
1 tbsp goldenberries
1 tbsp cranberries

1. Core and chop one pear and one apple. Place them in a serving bowl with half the banana and pour over half the apple juice and half the lemon juice. Stir well to combine.

2. Core, peel and roughly chop the remaining pear and apple. Add them to a blender with the rest of the banana.

3. Add the remaining apple juice and lemon juice to the blender with the sultanas and nuts. Blend until you have a finely chopped mixture.

4. Stir the blended mixture into the chopped fruit, along with the sunflower seeds, sugar and cinnamon. Scatter over the goldenberries and cranberries. Chill in the fridge if you have time, or serve immediately.

GOLDEN AND TANGY
Goldenberries are dried physalis – the small and tangy orange fruits you find for sale in late autumn.

PER SERVING: 438 KCALS | 7.5G FAT | 1G SAT FAT | 93.8G CARBS | 62.5G SUGARS | 14.6G FIBRE | 5.5G PROTEIN | TRACE SALT

VERY BERRY OVERNIGHT OATS

This is a perfect breakfast to bring to work as it's made in a lidded jar. Prepare your oats the night before and they'll be ready to eat or pick up with no fuss in the morning.

SERVES: 1
PREP: 5 MINS, PLUS SOAKING

40 g/1½ oz raw rolled oats
½ tbsp milled flaxseed
½ tbsp acai berry powder
2 tsp goji berries
1 tbsp flaked almonds
½ tbsp raw honey
125 ml/4 fl oz raw almond milk
2 tbsp blueberries
3 strawberries

1. Put the oats, flaxseed, acai berry powder, goji berries, most of the flaked almonds, the honey and almond milk in a lidded jar with a 225–250 ml/8–9 fl oz capacity. Stir well.

2. Stir a few of the blueberries into the oat mixture. Close the jar and chill in the fridge overnight.

3. In the morning, chop the strawberries. Top the oats with the remaining blueberries, strawberries and the remaining almonds.

BERRY ACAI
Acai berry powder is full of fibre, vitamin E, iron and calcium, and is very high in antioxidants.

PER SERVING: 437 KCALS | 21.5G FAT | 1.7G SAT FAT | 52.3G CARBS | 15.9G SUGARS | 11.1G FIBRE | 13.1G PROTEIN | TRACE SALT

BUCKWHEAT GRANOLA BARS

These gorgeous squares are packed with goodness and are very simple to make. Because they're rich in protein and healthy fats, they are a great way of keeping hunger at bay throughout the morning.

MAKES: 15 BARS
PREP: 15 MINS, PLUS SOAKING AND COOLING

1 tbsp melted cold-pressed extra virgin coconut oil, plus 2 tsp for brushing
60 g/2¼ oz raw rolled oats
50 g/1¾ oz ground almonds
50 g/1¾ oz sunflower seeds
30 g/1 oz pumpkin seeds
50 g/1¾ oz raw pistachio kernels
50 g/1¾ oz cacao nibs
30 g/1 oz goji berries
70 g/2½ oz raw buckwheat groats, soaked in water for 20 minutes, drained and rinsed
50 g/1¾ oz dried apricots, chopped
50 g/1¾ oz Medjool dates, stoned and chopped
2 tbsp raw almond butter
5 tbsp raw honey

1. Brush a 25 x 15–18-cm/10 x 6–7-inch dish with coconut oil and line it with enough baking paper to hang over the sides. Set aside.

2. In a large bowl, combine the oats, ground almonds, seeds, pistachio kernels, cacao nibs and goji berries, and stir well. Tip the soaked groats into the bowl and combine. Stir in the apricots and dates.

3. In a small bowl, combine the almond butter, honey and coconut oil. Warm on the lowest setting in the microwave for 1 minute, or in a small pan over gentle heat, and mix with a fork.

4. Pour the almond butter mixture over the dry ingredients and stir well so that everything is moist.

5. Tip the granola into the prepared dish and press it down firmly. Cover and refrigerate overnight, or for several hours, then remove from the dish using the over-hanging paper. Peel this off.

6. Cut the granola into 5-cm/2-inch bars using a sharp knife. Store them in a lidded container in the fridge.

STORAGE
The bars will store in an airtight container in the fridge for a week, or they can be frozen.

PER BAR: 180 KCALS | 9.6G FAT | 2.4G SAT FAT | 22.9G CARBS | 11.3G SUGARS | 4.2G FIBRE | 5.5G PROTEIN | TRACE SALT

NATURAL BLACKBERRY BARS

Two of nature's favourites, blackberries and hazelnuts, meet Caribbean coconut to make creamy bars with a crisp, nutty base. They are also full of vitamin C and healthy oils.

MAKES: 8 OBLONGS OR 16 SMALL SQUARES
PREP: 20 MINS, PLUS CHILLING

4 tbsp melted cold-pressed extra virgin coconut oil,
plus 1 tbsp for brushing
125 g/4½ oz raw coconut flour
40 g/1½ oz ground almonds
50 g/1¾ oz raw hazelnuts, chopped
30 g/1 oz raw almonds, chopped
1 tbsp raw sugar
3 tbsp maple syrup

TOPPING
175 g/6 oz blackberries
150 g/5½ oz strawberries
75 g/2½ oz raw coconut flour
juice of 1 lemon
100 ml/3½ fl oz raw coconut milk
4 tbsp raw creamed coconut
4 tbsp melted cold-pressed extra virgin coconut oil
4 tbsp maple syrup
2 tbsp cacao nibs

1. Brush a 20-cm/8-inch tin with coconut oil and line it with baking paper. Set aside.

2. To make the base, combine the coconut flour, ground almonds, nuts and sugar in a mixing bowl.

3. Gently warm the coconut oil with the maple syrup on the lowest setting in the microwave for 1 minute, or in a small pan over gentle heat. Stir the melted ingredients into the dry ones.

4. Press the mixture into the base of the prepared tin. Chill in the fridge for an hour, or until the mixture has hardened.

5. Meanwhile, make the topping. Blend the blackberries and strawberries in a blender, then blend in the coconut flour, lemon juice and coconut milk.

6. Gently warm the creamed coconut with the coconut oil and maple syrup, and combine well. Add to the ingredients in the blender and blend everything for a few seconds.

7. When the base has chilled, spoon the blackberry mixture evenly over the top. Cover and chill again for about 2 hours. The topping will not be very firm but should be firm enough to cut.

8. Grate cacao nibs over the top of the chilled mixture and cut it into 8 oblongs or 16 squares with a sharp knife.

TOP TOPPINGS
For a summertime spin on this recipe, try a mix of raspberries, redcurrants and strawberries.

PER SMALL SQUARE: 232 KCALS | 17G FAT | 11.4G SAT FAT | 17.2G CARBS | 7.4G SUGARS | 6.8G FIBRE | 3.8G PROTEIN | TRACE SALT

WAKE-UP SALAD

When you want something savoury for breakfast, try this crunchy salad.
It's layered with different fruits and vegetables, and is quick to put together!

SERVES: 2
PREP: 10 MINS

125 g/4½ oz kale, chopped
1 large red-skinned apple, cored and chopped
1 carrot, peeled and thinly sliced
4 Medjool dates, stoned and chopped
2 tbsp chopped raw walnuts
2 tsp sesame seeds
2 tsp hemp seeds
2 tsp sunflower seeds

DRESSING

3 tbsp cold-pressed extra virgin rapeseed oil
1 tbsp raw cider vinegar
2 tsp stone ground mustard
2 tsp maple syrup
½ tsp sea salt
½ tsp black pepper
2 spring onions, finely chopped

1. To make the dressing, combine the dressing ingredients in a lidded jar or small mixing bowl. Shake or stir well.

2. Tip the kale into a serving bowl, or two individual dishes. Add the apple and carrot, and stir in the dates and walnuts.

3. Pour the dressing over the salad and mix together. Sprinkle with the seeds to serve.

SEED HEALTH

Hemp seeds are a great source of antioxidants. This recipe has unhulled seeds for a richer mineral and fibre content, but you can also use hulled seeds – both are widely available.

PER SERVING: 555 KCALS | 31.9G FAT | 2.5G SAT FAT | 66.2G CARBS | 49.6G SUGARS | 10.1G FIBRE | 8.6G PROTEIN | 1.7G SALT

BEETROOT AND POMEGRANATE SMOOTHIE BOWL

*Tender beetroot and zesty pomegranate seeds are a fabulous combination.
The addition of spinach and wheatgrass makes this tasty breakfast bowl truly healthy.*

SERVES: 1
PREP: 10 MINS, PLUS OPTIONAL CHILLING

1 large beetroot, peeled and chopped
15 g/½ oz spinach leaves
3 tbsp pomegranate seeds
100 ml/3½ fl oz water
juice of 1 orange
1 tbsp raw honey
125 g/4½ oz raw yogurt
1 tsp wheatgrass powder
2 tsp buckwheat groats
2 round orange slices, halved

1. Put the beetroot in a blender with the spinach, 2 tablespoons of the pomegranate seeds and half the water. Blend until smooth.

2. Add the rest of the water, the orange juice, honey, 100 g/3½ oz yogurt and the wheatgrass powder to the blender. Blend again.

3. Pour the smoothie into a serving bowl and chill for an hour or so if you have time.

4. Drizzle the remaining yogurt over the smoothie. Sprinkle over the groats and decorate with the orange slices and remaining seeds.

RING THE CHANGES
Try raspberries instead of pomegranate seeds for a change, or if you want to make this smoothie when pomegranates aren't in season.

PER SERVING: 604 KCALS | 32.7G FAT | 28G SAT FAT | 75.7G CARBS | 48.6G SUGARS | 17.6G FIBRE | 10.2G PROTEIN | 0.4G SALT

MORNING POWER BOWL SMOOTHIE

Here's a great way to increase your nutrient intake, with lots of colourful fruits to provide antioxidants, and healthy fats from nuts and seeds.

SERVES: 1
PREP: 10 MINS

50 g/1³/₄ oz strawberries
50 g/1³/₄ oz blackberries
50 g/1³/₄ oz raspberries
1 banana, peeled
150 ml/5 fl oz hemp milk
1 tbsp coconut oil
1 tbsp ground almonds
1 kiwi, peeled and sliced
2 tsp chia seeds
1 small mango, peeled, stoned and chopped
1 tbsp chopped walnuts
2 tsp toasted sesame seeds

1. Place the strawberries, blackberries, raspberries, half the banana, the hemp milk, coconut oil and ground almonds in a blender and blend until smooth.

2. Pour into a bowl and place the remaining ingredients on top to serve.

TOP CHOICE

Replace the topping with fruits and nuts of your choice, aiming to use those in season – luscious berries would be great in the summer, sprinkled with freshly shredded mint leaves.

PER SERVING: 654 KCALS | 34.4G FAT | 13.8G SAT FAT | 86.9G CARBS | 51.1G SUGARS | 19.5G FIBRE | 11.1G PROTEIN | 0.1G SALT

MATCHA POWER SMOOTHIE

This is one of the best green smoothies you'll ever try — it's bursting with super ingredients, including spinach and avocado, to kick-start your day.

SERVES: 1
PREP: 5 MINS, PLUS OPTIONAL CHILLING

30 g/1 oz spinach
1 banana, peeled and chopped
1 small ripe avocado, peeled, stoned and roughly chopped
2 kiwi fruits, peeled and chopped
125 ml/4 fl oz raw almond milk
½ tbsp raw honey
1 tsp matcha tea powder
½ tsp wheatgrass powder
2 tsp flaked almonds, to decorate
½ tsp maca powder, to decorate

1. Blend the spinach, banana, avocado and one of the kiwi fruits in a blender with half the milk until you have a purée.

2. Add the honey, matcha, wheatgrass and remaining milk to the blender and blend until smooth. Pour the smoothie into your serving bowl. Chill for an hour if you have time.

3. Top your smoothie with the remaining kiwi and decorate with the flaked almonds and maca powder.

MAGICAL MATCHA
Matcha is a Japanese green tea rich in catechins, a type of antioxidant that fights cancers and heart disease. When you add matcha powder to a dish, you're getting the full benefit of the leaves rather than simply drinking a brew and discarding the leaves.

PER SERVING: 566 KCALS | 30.3G FAT | 3.3G SAT FAT | 72.1G CARBS | 37.4G SUGARS | 18.9G FIBRE | 13.2G PROTEIN | 0.1G SALT

POWER GULP

Beetroot is the favourite vegetable among sportsmen and sportswomen. It's great for boosting stamina and making muscles work harder, and is packed with vitamins, minerals, carbohydrates, protein and powerful antioxidants.

SERVES: 4
PREP: 5 MINUTES

2 beetroots, halved
30 g/1 oz flaxseeds (linseeds)
4 plums, stoned and quartered
150 g/5½ oz seedless red grapes
225 ml/8 fl oz chilled water
ice, to serve (optional)

1. Feed the beetroots through a juicer. Put the flaxseeds in a blender and whizz until finely ground. Add the beetroot juice, plums, grapes and water and whizz until smooth. Pour into four glasses, add ice (if using) and serve immediately.

BEETROOT POWER
Beetroot has one of the highest sugar levels of any vegetable, so it gives a great energy boost. It also helps regulate blood pressure and nerve function.

PER SERVING: 118 KCALS | 3.4G FAT | 0.3G SAT FAT | 21.2G CARBS | 15.8G SUGARS | 3.6G FIBRE | 2.9G PROTEIN | 0.1G SALT

LUNCHES AND SNACKS

SPRING ROLLS IN THE RAW

If you've never tried making your own spring rolls, you'll be delighted at how easy they are. These colourful rolls taste scrumptious and are packed with fibre and antioxidants.

MAKES: 16 HALF-ROLLS, TO SERVE 4
PREP: 15 MINS

8 round rice spring roll wrappers
1 sweet yellow pepper, halved, deseeded and thinly sliced
1 sweet red pepper, halved, deseeded and thinly sliced
½ cucumber, halved, deseeded and thinly sliced
1 pak choi, leaves separated and stalks sliced
2 carrots, peeled and cut into 10–cm/4-inch batons
4 large spring onions, sliced lengthways
2 celery stalks
2 tsp raw coconut aminos

COCONUT DIP

200 ml/7 fl oz raw coconut yogurt
2 tsp raw coconut aminos
½ tsp ground cumin seeds
½ tsp ground coriander seeds
½ garlic clove, crushed
½ tsp sea salt
3 tbsp chopped fresh coriander leaves

1. Soak a spring roll wrapper for 10 seconds, or until just pliable, then smooth it onto a working board. Arrange one eighth of all the vegetables onto the lower centre of the wrap. Sprinkle over a little of the coconut aminos.

2. Tuck each side of the wrapper into the centre, then fold the lower edge up to enclose the vegetables, keeping them in a tight bunch as you roll up to the top. Repeat with the remaining 7 wrappers.

3. Using a sharp knife, cut each roll in half until you have 16 halves and arrange them on a serving dish.

4. To make the dip, combine the yogurt in a mixing bowl with the coconut aminos, the cumin, coriander, garlic, salt and half the coriander leaves. Spoon the dip into a serving dish and serve alongside the spring rolls, garnished with the remaining coriander, if liked.

DIP THE CHANGES

For another occasion, try serving the rolls with a nutty dip – just swirl raw cashew butter into some nut milk and add a dash of raw coconut aminos.

PER SERVING: 266 KCALS | 13.2G FAT | 11.2G SAT FAT | 35G CARBS | 8.8G SUGARS | 7G FIBRE | 4.8G PROTEIN | 1.6G SALT

CHILLED BEETROOT AND WATERMELON SOUP

Bolstered by sweet flavours and a host of health-giving nutrients,
this soup tastes amazing all year round. Serve it chilled for
a summer gazpacho, or warmed during the frosty winter months.

SERVES: 4
PREP: 10 MINS, PLUS CHILLING

4 tender beetroots, about 600 g/1 lb 5 oz, peeled
1 large carrot, about 175 g/6 oz, peeled
300 g/10½ oz watermelon flesh
juice of ½ lemon
100 ml/3½ fl oz water
1 tsp sea salt
1 tsp black pepper
3 tbsp chopped fresh dill
150 g/5½ oz raw yogurt

1. Blend two thirds of the beetroot, carrot and watermelon in a blender with the lemon juice and most of the water until smooth. Add the salt and pepper and add the water, a little at a time, and blend again until you have a medium–thick soup texture. Pour the soup into a large bowl.

2. Grate the remaining beetroot and carrot, and stir into the soup. Chop the remaining watermelon into 1–cm/½–inch pieces and stir half of them into the soup with half the dill.

3. Pour the soup into four serving bowls and drizzle over the yogurt. Scatter the remaining watermelon pieces over the top and sprinkle over the rest of the dill. Chill in the fridge before serving.

PER SERVING: 209 KCALS | 9.9G FAT | 8.4G SAT FAT | 29.6G CARBS | 19G SUGARS | 8.5G FIBRE | 4.4G PROTEIN | 1.9G SALT

GARLIC AND HERB LABNEH

Labneh is a great dip to make using a simple coconut yogurt recipe that is left to drain overnight. You can add your own flavours with herbs and spices. It is a great source of fibre and healthy probiotics, which are important for gut health.

SERVES: 4

PREP: 30 MINUTES PLUS STANDING AND DRAINING TIME

60 ml/2 fl oz raw coconut water
300 g/10 oz fresh or frozen defrosted tender white coconut meat
1 probiotic powder capsule
1 clove garlic
2 tbsp mixed fresh soft herbs
2 tbsp extra virgin olive oil
2 tbsp pistachio nuts
400 g/14 oz freshly cut vegetable crudités including asparagus, red pepper, cucumber, baby courgette, baby corn, carrots and broccoli florets
salt and pepper (optional)

1. Process the coconut meat with half the coconut water until it is thoroughly blended. Then add the rest of the water and blend again until smooth.

2. Break open the probiotic capsules and sprinkle the powder contents into the blender; pulse for a few seconds.

3. Pour the mixture into a large wide necked jar. Put the lid on and leave the jar in a warm kitchen or room for up to 16 hours until you have a yogurt mixture.

4. Spoon the yogurt into a sieve lined with muslin, which is set over a bowl. Refrigerate for 24 hours or until the yogurt remaining in the sieve is of a consistency similar to very soft cheese. Discard any liquid in the bowl.

5. Stir the garlic and herbs into the labneh and season with salt and pepper, if using.

6. Divide between four bowls, drizzle with oil and sprinkle with chopped nuts. Serve with vegetable crudités for dipping.

PER SERVING: 380 KCALS | 34G FAT | 23.5G SAT FAT | 19G CARBS | 8.7G SUGARS | 9.4G FIBRE | 4.9G PROTEIN | 0.1G SALT

RAW SAUERKRAUT

Fermented foods, such as sauerkraut and kimchi, are beneficial for the digestive system as they're rich in good bacteria. This sauerkraut recipe is particularly easy and quick to make.

SERVES: 8
PREP: 10 MINS, PLUS FERMENTING

350 g/12 oz red cabbage, shredded
150 g/5½ oz white cabbage, shredded
100 g/3½ oz carrots, peeled and thinly sliced
4–cm/1½–inch piece fresh ginger, peeled and finely chopped
2½ tsp sea salt

1. Mix all the ingredients together in a large plastic mixing bowl.

2. Firmly knead the mixture for 5 minutes, until the vegetables begin to release their juice and become softer.

3. Pack the mixture into a lidded jar with a 700 ml/1¼ fl oz capacity. Press the top of the mixture down and top up with enough water to completely cover the vegetables.

4. Close the jar and keep it at room temperature for a week. Every day, open the jar and press the sauerkraut down again – you should see air bubbles coming out of the top of the mixture. Ensure all the vegetables are completely covered in the brine.

5. After a week, you can eat the sauerkraut, or store it in a cool place for several weeks.

BEETROOT BOOST
Try making a similar recipe using beetroot instead of carrot. You can also add spices such as caraway seeds or cumin to give the sauerkraut a little kick.

PER SERVING: 24 KCALS | 0.2G FAT | TRACE SAT FAT | 5.7G CARBS | 2.9G SUGARS | 1.8G FIBRE | 1G PROTEIN | 1.9G SALT

COOL CUCUMBER SUSHI

Who doesn't love a plateful of pretty sushi with tantalizing side dips? These rolls feature home-made cucumber wrappers, a colourful selection of vegetables and cauliflower rice.

MAKES: 16 SUSHI ROLLS, TO SERVE 4
PREP: 25 MINS

CUCUMBER SKIN SUSHI
1 x 30-cm/12-inch cucumber
100 g/3$\frac{1}{2}$ oz cauliflower florets
1 tsp cold-pressed extra virgin sesame oil
1 tsp raw rice vinegar
$\frac{1}{2}$ tsp salt
$\frac{1}{2}$ avocado, peeled
2 spring onions, finely chopped
$\frac{1}{2}$ small red pepper, finely chopped
sea salt (optional)

SPICY CASHEW DIP
70 g/2$\frac{1}{2}$ oz raw cashew nuts, soaked in water
for 1 hour, drained and rinsed
2 tsp finely chopped fresh ginger
2 tsp raw wasabi paste

CUCUMBER WRAPPERS
1 x 30-cm/12-inch cucumber
50 g/1$\frac{3}{4}$ oz baby spinach leaves
1 small courgette, finely sliced
1 carrot, finely sliced
4 tbsp raw cashew butter

MUSHROOM DRESSING
2 dark-gilled mushrooms, roughly chopped
1 tsp sea salt
50 ml/2 fl oz water
1 tsp finely chopped fresh ginger

1. Cut the top and tail off the cucumber so that you have a centre section that is one width. Cut into 8 pieces, 4 cm/1$\frac{1}{2}$ inches long. Scoop out the seed section and about half the flesh from each piece to form 8 hollow sushi rolls. Set aside.

2. Put the cauliflower, sesame oil, rice vinegar and salt in a food processor and pulse until the mixture resembles cooked rice.

3. Mash the avocado in a small bowl, adding salt to taste, if using.

4. Arrange your cucumber shapes on a board or serving platter and fill each one with some cauliflower rice, pressing it towards the sides. Add some avocado and press it into the rice. Sprinkle in some spring onions and red pepper.

5. To make the dip, put the soaked nuts in a food processor and process for several minutes until you have a creamy consistency. Beat in the ginger and wasabi paste, and transfer to a small serving dish.

6. Start making the cucumber wrappers. Top and tail the cucumber as before. Cut the cucumber in half, then cut each half into very thin strips lengthways and discard the first skin layer. You will need 24 strips for the 8 rolls.

7. To make each roll, arrange 3 cucumber strips on a board. Place one eighth of the spinach leaves at one end in a line from left to right. Arrange one eighth of the courgette and carrot slices on top, again in a line from left to right, and one eighth of the cashew cream.

8. Starting with the filled end, roll up the cucumber strip until you have a filled tube. Transfer the roll to a serving board or plate and continue to make the rest of the sushi.

9. To make the dressing, blend the mushrooms, salt and water in a clean processor until you have a smooth sauce. Add a little more water to make a soy sauce consistency and stir in the ginger. Serve in a small bowl alongside the sushi.

PER SERVING: 297 KCALS | 19.2G FAT | 3.2G SAT FAT | 27.2G CARBS | 9G SUGARS | 5.8G FIBRE | 10.1G PROTEIN | 2.5G SALT

JEWEL SALAD WITH RANCH DRESSING

A beautiful salad is always a welcome addition to the dinner table. This vibrant dish is complemented by a protein-rich variation of the classic American ranch dressing.

SERVES: 4
PREP: 20 MINS, PLUS SOAKING

2 large tomatoes, deseeded
1 cucumber
1/2 red onion
1 carrot
1 yellow pepper, deseeded
10 red radishes
8 tbsp mixed chopped soft herbs, such as parsley, mint and coriander
zest and juice of 1/2 lemon
4 tbsp cold-pressed extra virgin olive oil
1/2 tsp sea salt
1/2 tsp black pepper

RANCH DRESSING
100 g/3 1/2 oz raw cashew nuts, soaked in water for 2 hours, drained and rinsed
1 tbsp raw cider vinegar
125 ml/4 fl oz raw coconut milk
1 garlic clove, crushed
1/2 tsp sea salt
2 spring onions, finely chopped
2 tbsp chopped fresh parsley

1. To make the dressing, put the soaked nuts, vinegar, 50 ml/2 fl oz coconut milk, the garlic and salt in a blender. Blend until you have a smooth paste. Add milk a little at a time until you have a fairly thick mix. It should be a cross between a dip and a pouring consistency. Stir in the spring onions and parsley.

2. To make the salad, finely chop the vegetables and put them in a large serving bowl, or smaller individual ones. Stir in all the remaining salad ingredients and serve.

SYNC WITH THE SEASONS
You can vary the salad ingredients according to what you have, or what is in season. For example, try swapping the yellow pepper for sweetcorn kernels.

PER SERVING: 360 KCALS | 28.8G FAT | 7.2G SAT FAT | 22.7G CARBS | 9.4G SUGARS | 6G FIBRE | 7.5G PROTEIN | 1.5G SALT

CUCUMBER AND BUCKWHEAT YOGURT

Raw yogurt is a wonderful base for all kinds of savoury dishes. Make this crunchy and refreshing yogurt jar for an easy lunch or light bite on the go.

SERVES: 4
PREP: 10 MINS, PLUS SOAKING AND CHILLING

1 cucumber, halved, deseeded and chopped
500 g/1 lb 2 oz raw coconut yogurt
3 tbsp chopped fresh mint
1 tsp sea salt
1 tsp black pepper
100 g/3½ oz sun-dried raisins
70 g/2½ oz chopped raw walnuts
125 g/4½ oz raw buckwheat groats, soaked in water for 20 minutes, drained and rinsed
20 fresh mint leaves, to garnish

1. Wrap the cucumber pieces in kitchen paper and squeeze to release the moisture – the kitchen paper should end up soaked.

2. Mix the yogurt, mint, salt and pepper together in a bowl.

3. Divide the ingredients evenly between four lidded jars with a 250–275 g/9 oz–9¾ oz capacity. Layer with the raisins, half the walnuts, the soaked groats, three quarters of the cucumber and the yogurt mixture. Garnish with the remaining cucumber and walnuts.

4. Divide the mint leaves between each of the jars and chill for 30 minutes before serving.

INGREDIENT SWAPS
Try finely chopped spring onions instead of the mint and add half a teaspoon of crushed garlic to the yogurt mixture. Fresh, green, new season's garlic is best.

PER SERVING: 659 KCALS | 45G FAT | 29.3G SAT FAT | 63.4G CARBS | 23.6G SUGARS | 15.2G FIBRE | 12G PROTEIN | 1.6G SALT

AUBERGINE, LETTUCE AND AVOCADO SANDWICH

*When you fancy a satisfying raw lunch, you'll fall in love with this sandwich.
It's filled with creamy cashew cheese, smashed avocado and crisp slices of aubergine.*

MAKES: 2 SANDWICHES
PREP: 25 MINS, PLUS SOAKING, MARINATING AND DEHYDRATING

CRISPY AUBERGINE
1 large aubergine
2 tbsp cold-pressed extra virgin olive oil
1 tbsp raw agave nectar
1 tbsp raw coconut aminos
2 tsp minced fresh red mild chilli
1/3 tsp sea salt

CASHEW CHEESE
70 g/2 1/2 oz raw cashew nuts, soaked in water
for 1 hour, drained and rinsed
2 garlic cloves
1 tbsp lemon juice
2 tsp raw coconut aminos
1/3 tsp sea salt

RED PEPPER PESTO
1 small red pepper, roughly chopped
15 g/1 oz sun-dried tomatoes, soaked in water for 10
minutes, drained and rinsed
30 g/1 oz raw pine nuts
1/4 tsp sea salt and 1/4 tsp black pepper

SMASHED AVOCADO
1 ripe avocado, stoned and peeled
1 spring onion, chopped
juice of 1/2 lime and 1/4 tsp sea salt
1/4 tsp black pepper
1 tbsp chopped fresh coriander leaves

4 Little Gem lettuce leaves, to serve
1 tomato, sliced, to serve

1. You will need a dehydrator for this recipe. If you don't have a dehydrator, many electric cookers will dehydrate food on a low enough heat (the dehydrate high setting is 60°C/140°F; the dehydrate low setting is 45°C/115°F). This may be the defrost setting or slightly higher, or a designated dehydrate setting. Check you have the correct temperature with an oven thermometer before dehydrating in a standard cooker.

2. Slice the aubergine into 8 long slices, about 5 mm/1/4 inch thick, and discard the two skin sides. Combine the rest of the ingredients in a small bowl and brush each aubergine slice with the mixture.

3. Put the aubergine in a non-metallic dish and cover. Leave to marinate for 2 hours, then drain and layer on a dehydrator tray. (If using the oven, use a non-stick oven tray.) Dehydrate on low (45°C/115°F) for 8 hours, turning the slices halfway.

4. Meanwhile, make the cashew cheese. Blend the soaked nuts in a food processor with the remaining ingredients until you have a smooth paste. Thin with a little water if necessary and blend again. Remove the cheese from the processor and set aside in a bowl.

5. Make the red pepper pesto. Add the red pepper, soaked tomatoes, pine nuts, and salt and pepper to a processor and pulse until you have a thick paste with small visible pieces in it.

6. Before you assemble your sandwiches, make the smashed avocado. In a small bowl, mash the avocado flesh with the rest of the ingredients until you have a textured purée.

7. Prepare your sandwiches on your serving plates. For each sandwich, start with two slices of aubergine side by side. Top with half the cashew cheese and two lettuce leaves. Smooth on half the red pepper pesto and arrange half the tomato slices on top. Add half the avocado mixture and smooth down, then finish with two more aubergine slices. Serve immediately.

PER SERVING: 725 KCALS | 51.4G FAT | 7G SAT FAT | 62.5G CARBS | 31.5G SUGARS | 19.2G FIBRE | 16.4G PROTEIN | 3.6G SALT

VEGETABLE FRIES WITH CASHEW DIP

Forget about potato fries – once you try this mouth-watering raw version with their truly delicious dip, you'll want to make them time and again.

SERVES: 2
PREP: 20 MINS, PLUS SOAKING AND DEHYDRATING

1 small butternut squash
1 courgette, about 250 g/9 oz, cut into thin batons
1 tbsp cold-pressed extra virgin rapeseed oil
½ tsp sea salt
½ tsp black pepper

CASHEW DIP

70 g/2½ oz raw cashew nuts, soaked in water for 2 hours, drained and rinsed
2 tbsp raw tahini
1 tbsp lemon juice
1 garlic clove, crushed
1 carrot, peeled and chopped
¼ tsp sea salt
¼ tsp black pepper
50 ml/1¾ fl oz raw almond milk

1. You will need a dehydrator for this recipe. If you don't have a dehydrator, many electric cookers will dehydrate food on a low enough heat (the dehydrate high setting is 60°C/140°F; the dehydrate low setting is 45°C/115°F). This may be the defrost setting or slightly higher, or a designated dehydrate setting. Check you have the correct temperature with an oven thermometer before dehydrating in a standard cooker.

2. Cut the squash in half between the thinner end and bulbous base. Reserve the bulbous base for another dish. Peel the squash and cut it into thin batons.

3. Toss the courgette and squash batons with the rapeseed oil, salt and pepper, and arrange them on a dehydrator tray. If using the oven use a non-stick oven tray.) Dehydrate on high (60°C/140°F) for an hour, then low (45°C/115°F) for 8 hours, turning the batons halfway.

4. Meanwhile, make the cashew dip. Add the soaked nuts to a blender with the tahini and lemon juice, and process until you have a rough butter.

5. Add the garlic, carrot, salt and pepper to the blender and process again until you have a pâté consistency. Remove the mixture and stir in the nut milk a little at a time until you have a dip-like consistency – you may not need all the milk, or you may need a little more.

6. When the batons are crispy and fry-like, remove them from the dehydrator and serve with the dip.

SWEET POTATO FRIES
You can make these fries with sweet potato instead of the squash or courgettes.

PER SERVING: 473 KCALS | 33.2G FAT | 4.6G SAT FAT | 39.6G CARBS | 9.8G SUGARS | 8.1G FIBRE | 12.9G PROTEIN | 2.3G SALT

MISO SOUP WITH RADISH AND SPROUTED SEEDS

Miso soup is a cherished dish eaten in Japan every day. Made from fermented soybeans, miso is the perfect base for a raw soup as it's rich in protein and beneficial bacteria.

SERVES: 4
PREP: 12 MINS, PLUS SPROUTING

2 tbsp shell-on sunflower seeds suitable for sprouting
2½ tbsp organic miso paste
1 large garlic clove
2 tsp finely chopped fresh ginger
1½ tbsp raw rice vinegar
50 ml/1¾ fl oz water
3 spring onions
12 mangetout
4 radishes
8 baby sweetcorn cobs
75 g/2½ oz fresh coconut shards
30 g/1 oz pea shoots
1 tbsp cold-pressed extra virgin sesame oil, to serve

1. Start sprouting the sunflower seeds 3 days before you want to make the soup. Put them in a shallow dish lined with plenty of thick kitchen paper. Sprinkle tepid water over the seeds and cover with more paper. Sprinkle again. Leave in a warm room in the dark. Check each day that the seeds are still slightly damp. When they begin to sprout, remove the top layer of paper and bring into the light. The sprouts can be eaten when they are about 8 mm/³⁄₈ inch long.

2. To make the soup, blend the miso paste with the garlic, ginger, rice vinegar and water in a blender. Add more water until you have 1.2 litres/2 pints and stir well. Pour the soup into four bowls.

3. Thinly slice the spring onions, mangetout, radishes and sweetcorn, and arrange over the soup. Top with the coconut shards, pea shoots and sprouted seeds. Drizzle over the sesame oil to serve.

MISO PASTE
Buy organic, unpasteurized miso paste – some brands are pasteurized, which means the miso is heated above the minimal heat allowed on raw diets.

Note: recipes using sprouting seeds should be avoided by children younger than five, older adults, pregnant women and those with weakened immune systems, who are particularly vulnerable to the bacteria that may be present on sprouts.

PER SERVING: 156 KCALS | 11.9G FAT | 6.3G SAT FAT | 9.8G CARBS | 3.5G SUGARS | 3.7G FIBRE | 3.7G PROTEIN | 1G SALT

VEGETABLE AND SEED CRACKERS

This recipe makes clever use of the leftover pulp from juicing your vegetables – so no need to waste all that fibre and goodness! Nibble on one for breakfast or an afternoon snack.

MAKES: 16 CRACKERS
PREP: 10 MINS, PLUS SOAKING AND DEHYDRATING

300 g/10½ oz carrots, peeled and roughly chopped
150 g/5½ oz celery, roughly chopped
100 g/3½ oz red radishes, chopped
2 tbsp milled flaxseed
1 tbsp whole golden flaxseeds
3 tbsp sunflower seeds
1 tbsp pumpkin seeds
1¼ tsp sea salt
1½ tsp black pepper
1 tbsp chia seeds, soaked in 3 tbsp water
for 1 hour

1. You will need a dehydrator for this recipe. If you don't have a dehydrator, many electric cookers will dehydrate food on a low enough heat (the dehydrate high setting is 60°C/140°F; the dehydrate low setting is 45°C/115°F). This may be the defrost setting or slightly higher, or a designated dehydrate setting. Check you have the correct temperature with an oven thermometer before dehydrating in a standard cooker.

2. Juice the carrots, celery and radish, and save the juice to drink. Remove the pulp from the juicer and put it into a mixing bowl. You should have about 1 and a half mugfuls of pulp.

3. Stir the rest of the ingredients into the mixing bowl, including the soaked seeds and their water. Combine thoroughly, adding a little water if the mix seems very dry or doesn't stick together well.

4. Spread the mixture thinly and evenly on a dehydrator tray lined with a non-stick sheet. (If using the oven, use a non-stick oven tray.) Dehydrate on low (45°C/115°F) for 4 hours. Turn the mixture over, score it into 16 crackers and dehydrate on low for a further 4 hours, or until the crackers are crisped to your liking.

5. Allow the crackers to cool, then break along the knife scores. Store the crackers in an airtight container.

JUICING PROCESS

If you don't have a juicer, you can make the vegetable pulp by pulsing the vegetables in a processor, then simply squeezing the juice from the mix with clean hands. Alternatively, put the mix in a sieve over a bowl and bash firmly with a pestle or the round end of a rolling pin until the pulp is dry.

PER CRACKER: 29 KCALS | 2.1G FAT | 0.2G SAT FAT | 2.3G CARBS | 0.4G SUGARS | 1.3G FIBRE | 1.1G PROTEIN | 0.5G SALT

1 x 20g/¾ oz pack of mixed dried seaweed, soaked in
water for 5–10 minutes
1 large spring onion, finely chopped
1 red radish, finely chopped
2 tsp sesame seeds, to garnish

DRESSING

1 tbsp cold-pressed extra virgin sesame oil
1 tbsp raw rice vinegar
1 tbsp raw coconut aminos
1 tsp chopped red chilli
2 tsp mirin
1 tsp organic miso paste

1. While the seaweed is soaking, make the dressing. Add the sesame oil, rice vinegar, coconut aminos, chilli, mirin and miso paste to a small bowl and stir vigorously, to combine.

2. Once the seaweed is tender and reconstituted, drain it thoroughly in a colander and rinse.

3. Divide the seaweed between two shallow bowls and drizzle the dressing over it, tossing lightly.

4. Sprinkle the onion and radish over the salad and garnish with the sesame seeds to serve.

ALL SORTS OF SEAWEED

Dried seaweed mixes are widely available in health food shops and online. Some kinds you can try are wakame, dulse, agar agar, miyoek, chondrus, gigartina and kelp.

PER SERVING: 137 KCALS | 9.2G FAT | 1.4G SAT FAT | 8.2G CARBS | 2.5G SUGARS | 1.1G FIBRE | 11.6G PROTEIN | 0.5G SALT

OAT BREAD WITH CHIA SEEDS

Following a raw diet doesn't mean giving up bread.
For a delicious and extremely nutritious snack, you can make
this savoury oat, seed and nut loaf smattered with green olives.

MAKES: 1 LOAF (AROUND 12 SLICES)
PREP: 10 MINS, PLUS SOAKING AND DEHYDRATING

60 g/2¼ oz raw rolled oats
60 g/2¼ oz raw oatmeal
100 g/3½ oz buckwheat flour
50 g/1¾ oz pumpkin seeds
70 g/2½ oz raw walnuts, ground
30 g/1 oz ground psyllium husks
8 green olives, stoned and sliced
2 tsp sun-dried herbes de Provence (or half-dried
parsley and half-dried rosemary)
1 tsp sea salt
½ tsp black pepper
1 tbsp cold-pressed extra virgin rapeseed oil
2 tbsp chia seeds, soaked in 100 ml/3½ fl oz water
for 20 minutes

1. You will need a dehydrator for this recipe. If you don't have a dehydrator, many electric cookers will dehydrate food on a low enough heat (the dehydrate high setting is 60°C/140°F; the dehydrate low setting is 45°C/115°F). This may be the defrost setting or slightly higher, or a designated dehydrate setting. Check you have the correct temperature with an oven thermometer before dehydrating in a standard cooker.

2. Combine the oats, oatmeal, buckwheat flour, pumpkin seeds, ground walnuts and psyllium in a large mixing bowl. Stir in the olives, herbs, salt, pepper and rapeseed oil. Mix thoroughly.

3. Add the soaked chia seeds and their water to the mixing bowl and knead the mix. If the dough doesn't come together, add a tablespoon of water and knead again. Repeat if necessary. Four tablespoons of water should be enough to make a fairly dry dough.

4. On a board, form the dough into an oblong shape and transfer to a non-stick dehydrator sheet. (If using the oven, use a non-stick oven tray.) Using a sharp knife, score slices along the bread, cutting two thirds of the way into the loaf.

5. Place the sheet on a dehydrator tray and dehydrate on high for an hour (60°C/140°F), then turn to low (45°C/115°F) and continue dehydrating for 6 hours. Cut slices along the scores you made and dehydrate for a further hour on low, or until you have firm slices.

6. Store the oat bread in an airtight container.

SWAP THE NUTS

Walnuts provide a richness and depth of flavour
but you can substitute them with ground
Brazil nuts or ground hazelnuts.

PER SLICE: 163 KCALS | 9.3G FAT | 1.1G SAT FAT | 17.4G CARBS | 0.4G SUGARS | 5.4G FIBRE | 5G PROTEIN | 0.6G SALT

SEEDBURST FLATBREADS

These moreish, lightly dehydrated flatbreads are so easy to make and are bursting with nuts, seeds and an array of vegetables.

MAKES: 8 FLATBREADS
PREP: 10 MINS, PLUS DEHYDRATING

2 tbsp milled flaxseed
2 tbsp hulled hemp seeds
5 tbsp sunflower seeds
2 tbsp raw walnuts
1 tbsp raw rolled oats
1 courgette, peeled and roughly chopped (about 125 g/4½ oz peeled weight)
1 small carrot, peeled and roughly chopped
1 large celery stick, chopped
50 g/1¾ oz baby sweetcorn cobs
100 g/3½ oz red pepper, chopped
1 tbsp cold-pressed extra virgin rapeseed oil
1 tsp sea salt

1. You will need a dehydrator for this recipe.

2. Put the flaxseed and hemp seeds in a mixing bowl with 3 tablespoons of the sunflower seeds.

3. Grind the rest of the sunflower seeds, the walnuts and oats in a food processor and tip into the mixing bowl. Add the courgette, carrot, celery and sweetcorn to the processor and pulse until they are finely chopped. Add the red pepper and pulse for a second or two.

4. Tip the vegetable mixture into the bowl and stir in the rapeseed oil and salt. Add 1 or 2 tablespoons of water if the mix seems a bit dry. Stir again.

5. Transfer the mixture to two non-stick dehydrator sheets on dehydrator trays and press down to about 5 mm–8 mm/ ¼–⅜ inch thick. Dehydrate on high (60°C/140°F) for an hour, then turn to low (45°C/115°F) and dehydrate for a further 2–3 hours, or until the flatbread feels fairly dry to the touch.

6. Flip the flatbread over with a large flat spatula and score with a sharp knife to make 8 large squares. Dehydrate on low for a further 2–3 hours, or until the mixture is dry but still has some give – you want flatbread, not crackers!

7. Break or cut the flatbreads along the scores you made. Allow them to cool completely, then store in an airtight tin.

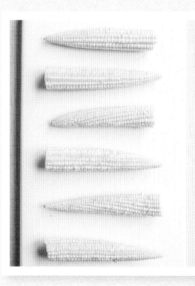

SERVING IDEA
Try a flatbread topped with slices of tomato and avocado, or raw cashew butter and cucumber.

PER FLATBREAD: 102 KCALS | 8G FAT | 0.7G SAT FAT | 5.1G CARBS | 1.9G SUGARS | 2.2G FIBRE | 3.3G PROTEIN | 0.8G SALT

MAINS

CUCUMBER NOODLE BOWL
WITH THAI DRESSING

This spicy Thai salad is a great source of cholesterol-lowering foods, such as beetroot, kale and seaweed. It also features a yummy peanut topping for a healthy heart.

SERVES: 2
PREP: 15 MINS

1 beetroot, peeled and spiralized
½ cucumber, spiralized
70 g/2½ oz kale, chopped
½ red onion, thinly sliced
1 small carrot, peeled and thinly sliced
40 g/1½ oz raw peanuts
2 tsp ground red seaweed
20 g/¾ oz fresh coconut flakes, to garnish
1 tbsp fresh coriander leaves, to garnish

DRESSING
2 tbsp cold-pressed extra virgin sesame oil
2 tsp organic miso paste
juice of ½ lime
1-cm/½-inch piece of fresh ginger, minced
1 large garlic clove, minced
1 small red chilli, minced
2 tsp raw peanut butter
salt (optional)

1. Arrange all but a few strands of the beetroot in two serving bowls. Add all of the cucumber strands.

2. Add the kale to the bowls and top with the onion and carrot.

3. To make the dressing, combine all the ingredients in a small bowl and mix well. Spoon this over the beetroot salad.

4. Run the peanuts under cold water, then pat them dry so they are just slightly damp. On a plate, roll them in the seaweed until they are thoroughly coated and sprinkle over the salad.

5. Add the coconut flakes and coriander leaves to the salad. Garnish with the remaining beetroot strands to serve.

NUTTY ADDITIONS
You can use raw peanut butter or raw cashew butter in the dressing and you can choose either of these nuts for the garnish.

PER SERVING: 409 KCALS | 30.4G FAT | 6.7G SAT FAT | 29.1G CARBS | 12.1G SUGARS | 8.4G FIBRE | 11.5G PROTEIN | 0.7G SALT

CAULIFLOWER SALAD WITH APPLE AND NUTS

Raw cauliflower, with its mild, slightly nutty flavour, tastes wonderful mixed with crisp spirals of apple, a scattering of walnuts and a fabulous tangy dressing.

SERVES: 4
PREP: 15 MINS

1 cauliflower, divided into small florets
1 large red-skinned dessert apple, cored and chopped
2 tbsp sunflower seeds
1 tbsp sesame seeds
3 tbsp chopped raw walnuts
1 large sweet potato, peeled and spiralized
1 small red onion, spiralized
1 tbsp cold-pressed extra virgin rapeseed oil
½ tsp sea salt
¼ tsp black pepper
2 tsp chopped fresh dill, to garnish

DRESSING

3 tbsp raw coconut yogurt
juice of ½ lemon
2 tsp grated fresh horseradish
1 tbsp chopped fresh dill
1 garlic clove, crushed
½ tsp sea salt
½ tsp black pepper

1. Put the cauliflower florets in a large bowl. Add three quarters of the apple, all of the seeds and 2 tablespoons of the walnuts.

2. Beat all the dressing ingredients together in a small bowl and pour over the cauliflower mix. Stir well until everything is coated.

3. Divide the sweet potato spirals between four serving dishes and sprinkle the onion spirals on top. Drizzle over the rapeseed oil, then add the salt and pepper.

4. Spoon the cauliflower mixture into the serving dishes. Top with the remaining apple and walnuts, and garnish with the dill to serve.

PER SERVING: 263 KCALS | 14.2G FAT | 3.6G SAT FAT | 30.8G CARBS | 12.4G SUGARS | 7.5G FIBRE | 7.1G PROTEIN | 1.7G SALT

RAW VEGETABLE LASAGNE

There are several elements to this gorgeous raw vegan lasagne,
but it really is quite easy to put together and is ideal for a dinner party.

SERVES: 2
PREP: 1HR 30 MINS

COURGETTE LAYER
225 g/8 oz courgettes, thinly sliced lengthways
½ tbsp olive oil
2 tsp balsamic vinegar
¼ tsp salt

NUT CHEESE LAYER
100 g/3½ oz shelled macadamia nuts
½ small yellow pepper, diced
1 tbsp nutritional yeast flakes
1½ tbsp lemon juice
¼ tsp salt

TOMATO SAUCE
2 tbsp tomato purée
½ tsp garlic purée
¼ tsp smoked paprika
½ tsp salt (optional)

AVOCADO PESTO
40 g/1½ oz pine nuts
1 large ripe avocado, roughly chopped
3 tbsp fresh basil leaves
1 small garlic clove, crushed
juice of ½ lime
¼ tsp salt

TOMATO AND SPINACH
2 large tomatoes, sliced
30 g/1 oz baby spinach leaves, de-stalked
2 tsp pine nuts, toasted, to garnish
2 tsp basil leaves, to garnish

1. To make the courgette layer, place the courgettes in a dish that will hold the slices in one layer. Cover the slices with the oil, vinegar and salt, ensuring that each slice is well covered, then set aside for up to 1 hour to soften and absorb the flavours.

2. To make the cheese layer, pulse all the ingredients except the salt in a blender until you have a smooth, light paste.

3. To make the tomato sauce, combine all the ingredients in a small bowl and then add approximately 2 tablespoons of cold water and mix thoroughly. Add a little more water until you have a pouring consistency. Add salt, if using.

4. To make the avocado pesto layer, put the pine nuts in an electric chopper or blender and process for a few seconds, or until chopped but not puréed. Add the avocado chunks, basil leaves, garlic, lime juice and salt and pulse until you have a lightly textured mixture.

5. Slice the tomatoes so that you have six inside slices from each. Discard the outer slices.

6. Layer up the two lasagne directly onto plates. Arrange a quarter of the courgette slices in a rectangle on the centre of each plate. For each plate, top with a quarter of the spinach leaves, then spoon on a quarter of the nut cheese. Add a quarter of the tomato slices and top those with a quarter of the avocado pesto. For each plate, add another quarter of the tomato slices, quarter of the cheese, quarter of the spinach, and quarter of the avocado pesto.

7. Finish by placing the remaining courgette slices on top of each lasagne. Drizzle the tomato sauce over the two lasagne and garnish with toasted pine nuts and basil leaves.

PER SERVING: 799 KCALS | 72.6G FAT | 9.9G SAT FAT | 37.8G CARBS | 14.1G SUGARS | 16.5G FIBRE | 15.1G PROTEIN | 2.3G SALT

AVOCADO HERO SALAD

This salad is full of gorgeous textures, contrasting creamy avocado with crunchy asparagus tips, and is rich in heart-healthy monounsaturated fats, soluble fibre and vitamin E.

SERVES: 2
PREP: 10 MINS, PLUS SPROUTING

85 g/3 oz dry green peas suitable for sprouting
85 g/3 oz whole quinoa seeds suitable for sprouting
70 g/2½ oz baby spinach
70 g/2½ oz baby asparagus tips
16 baby plum tomatoes
30 g/1 oz fresh watercress
2 ripe avocados, stoned, peeled and sliced into bite-sized pieces
2 tbsp raw pine nuts
8 fresh basil sprigs
½ tbsp cold-pressed extra virgin olive oil

DRESSING

2 tbsp cold-pressed extra virgin olive oil
½ tbsp raw wine vinegar
2 tsp raw honey
1 tsp stoneground mustard
½ tsp sea salt
½ tsp pepper

1. To sprout the peas, put them in a wide-necked glass jar and soak them overnight in tepid water, covered with muslin or a similar material. In the morning, drain and rinse the peas and fill the jar with fresh water. Drain and rinse the peas twice a day for 5 days, until they have sprouted. Rinse and drain to use.

2. To sprout the quinoa, use the same method as the peas but soak them for only 4 hours. They will sprout in about 2 days.

3. Arrange the spinach, all but 4 of the asparagus tips and the plum tomatoes in two serving dishes with most of the watercress.

4. Arrange three quarters of the avocado slices in the dishes with the remaining watercress and the sprouted peas and quinoa. Sprinkle three quarters of the pine nuts on top.

5. In a small bowl, mash the remaining avocado with the remaining pine nuts, 6 of the basil sprigs and the half-tablespoon of olive oil until you have a rough purée.

6. Make the dressing by thoroughly combining the ingredients in a small dish. Spoon most of this over the salad.

7. Finish the salad by arranging 2 asparagus tips in the centre of each dish, followed by half the avocado purée and a basil sprig. Drizzle over the rest of the dressing to serve.

WHY NOT TRY?
You can use flaked almonds or chopped hazelnuts if you don't have any pine nuts.

PER SERVING: 813 KCALS | 48.5G FAT | 6.2G SAT FAT | 80.6G CARBS | 13.3G SUGARS | 27.1G FIBRE | 23.4G PROTEIN | 1.6G SALT

FRUIT AND VEGETABLE KEBABS

*When you want something fresh, zingy and packed with vitamin C
and antioxidants, these kebabs are the perfect supper.*

SERVES: 4
PREP: 10 MINS, PLUS MARINATING

1 small Florence fennel bulb, split into leaves
1 small turnip, peeled and thinly sliced
50 g/1¾ oz butternut squash, peeled and thinly sliced
1 yellow pepper, deseeded and cut into squares
1 papaya, peeled, deseeded and cut into cubes
½ mango, peeled and cut into chunks
8 ready-prepared fresh coconut chunks

MARINADE
2 tbsp cold-pressed extra virgin olive oil
2 tsp raw agave nectar
2 tbsp orange juice
1 tbsp raw coconut aminos
½ tsp sea salt
½ tsp black pepper

SALAD
125 g/4½ oz fresh herb and salad leaves, such as
sorrel, mizuna, flat-leaf parsley, coriander and celery
2 tsp poppy seeds
2 tbsp raw yogurt
75 ml/2½ fl oz raw coconut milk
1 tbsp raw cider vinegar
1 garlic clove, crushed
½ tsp sea salt

1. You will need four wooden skewers for this recipe.

2. To make the kebabs, put all the fruit and vegetables in a non-metallic dish and mix well.

3. In a small bowl, combine the marinade ingredients and pour them over the kebab mixture. Stir well, cover and set aside for 3–5 hours.

4. Shake any excess marinade off the fruit and vegetables, and thread them onto four wooden skewers.

5. Arrange the salad leaves on four serving plates and sprinkle over the poppy seeds. Combine the yogurt, coconut milk, vinegar, garlic and salt in a separate small bowl and drizzle over the salad.

6. Serve the kebabs alongside the salad.

TURNIP SUBSTITUTIONS
If you can find it, salsify or mooli (white radish)
make great alternatives to the turnip.

PER SERVING: 285 KCALS | 18.8G FAT | 10.7G SAT FAT | 29.3G CARBS | 18.6G SUGARS | 7.4G FIBRE | 3.5G PROTEIN | 1.6G SALT

SEAWEED POWER BOWL

Seaweed is an extraordinary source of a nutrient missing in almost every other food – iodine. This is critically important to maintaining a healthy thyroid. A small serving of seaweed just once a week is recommended.

SERVES: 4
PREP: 20 MINS

10 g/¼ oz dried kelp
½ cucumber
2 oranges
1 red chilli, deseeded and finely diced
2 carrots, grated
1 large mango, peeled, stoned and chopped
3 heads of pak choi, chopped
15 g/½ oz fresh mint leaves
15 g/½ oz fresh coriander leaves
2 tbsp salted peanuts, chopped

DRESSING
3 tbsp olive oil
grated zest and juice of 1 lime
1 tsp clear honey
1 tsp miso paste

1. Place the kelp in a bowl of water and leave to stand for 10 minutes to rehydrate.

2. Meanwhile, to make the dressing, whisk together the oil, lime zest and juice, honey and miso paste.

3. Halve the cucumber lengthways and, using a teaspoon, scoop out and discard the seeds.

4. Peel the oranges and cut them into segments.

5. Roughly chop the kelp and place in a large bowl with the cucumber, orange segments, chilli, carrot, mango, pak choi and half the mint and coriander.

6. Pour in the dressing and toss well. Divide between four bowls.

7. Sprinkle each bowl with chopped peanuts and the remaining mint and coriander.

WHY NOT TRY?

If you can't find dried kelp, substitute with nori sheets that can be served dry, broken into shards, to add an extra crunch to the salad.

PER SERVING: 259 KCALS | 13.5G FAT | 1.9G SAT FAT | 32G CARBS | 22.2G SUGARS | 7.4G FIBRE | 5.3G PROTEIN | 0.4G SALT

SWEET-AND-SOUR 'STIR-FRY'

This attractive, Asian-inspired bowl is filled with goodies — raw kelp noodles are very low in carbs and calories, and oriental mushrooms can help regulate the immune system.

SERVES: 2
PREP: 15 MINS, PLUS SPROUTING AND SOAKING

40 g/1½ oz aduki beans suitable for sprouting
40 g/1½ oz mung beans suitable for sprouting
125 g/4½ oz parsnips, peeled and roughly chopped
125 g/4½ oz sweet potato, peeled and roughly chopped
1½ tbsp dried shiitake
mushrooms, soaked in water for 15 minutes, drained and rinsed
200 g/7 oz raw kelp noodles
50 g/1¾ oz pak choi, sliced
50 g/1¾ oz enoki mushrooms
1 mild red chilli, deseeded and finely sliced
30 g/1 oz raw pine nuts

CHILLI SAUCE
1 small, medium-hot red chilli, deseeded and chopped
1 tsp peeled and chopped fresh ginger
1 tbsp raw coconut aminos
2 tsp raw agave nectar
1 tbsp cold-pressed extra virgin sesame oil
1 tsp raw tahini
juice of ½ lime
2 tsp raw rice vinegar

1. Start sprouting the aduki and mung beans 3 days before you want to make the stir-fry. Put the beans in a wide-necked glass jar and soak them overnight in tepid water, covered with muslin or a similar material. In the morning, drain and rinse the beans and fill the jar with fresh water. Drain and rinse them twice a day for 3 days, until they have sprouted. Rinse and drain to use.

2. To make the stir-fry sauce, process all the ingredients until you have a paste. Add a little water until you have a thick pouring consistency and stir well.

3. Put the parsnips in a food processor and process until you have rice-sized pieces. Transfer to a mixing bowl. Do the same with the sweet potato and then lightly mix the two vegetables.

4. Chop the soaked shiitake mushrooms into small pieces and mix them into the vegetable rice.

5. Rinse the kelp noodles and shake to dry in a sieve. Arrange most of them in two serving bowls and top with the vegetable rice mixture.

6. Arrange the pak choi and enoki mushrooms on top of the rice, then dot spoonfuls of the sauce around the dish.

7. Finish with the chilli slices, pine nuts and sprouted beans. Finally arrange the few remaining kelp noodles on top and serve.

RICE ALTERNATIVES
You can use cauliflower instead of the parsnip to make your rice, and you can vary the type of sprouted seeds you use. Sprouted lentils and chickpeas are great alternatives.

PER SERVING: 489 KCALS | 19.2G FAT | 2G SAT FAT | 69.2G CARBS | 14.8G SUGARS | 14.1G FIBRE | 12.5G PROTEIN | 0.3G SALT

RAW SHOOTS AND SEEDS SUPER SALAD

Raw shoots and seeds are superfoods because the sprouting process increases the proportion of protein and fibre within each seedling, and gives them a lower glycemic index. They are always best eaten fresh.

SERVES: 6
PREP: 20 MINUTES

225 g/8 oz mixed sprouted seeds and beans (such as alfalfa, mung beans, soy beans, aduki beans, chickpeas and radish seeds)
30 g/1 oz pumpkin seeds
30 g/1 oz sunflower seeds
30 g/1 oz sesame seeds
1 small apple
70 g/2½ oz dried apricots
grated rind and juice of 1 lemon
50 g/1¾ oz walnuts, roughly chopped
2 tbsp vegan omega-rich oil

1. In a large mixing bowl, combine the sprouts and seeds. Core and chop the apple and chop the apricots into small pieces. Stir the fruit into the bowl, then stir in the lemon rind and walnuts.

2. Make a dressing by mixing the lemon juice with the oil in a small bowl using a fork to thoroughly combine.

3. Stir the dressing into the salad and serve immediately.

SPROUTING

Lentils, peas, aduki beans, mung beans and chickpeas are easy to sprout – sprouting will take between 4–8 days. Only consume them after they have sprouted when the natural toxins have broken down.

Note: recipes using sprouting seeds should be avoided by children younger than five, older adults, pregnant women and those with weakened immune systems, who are particularly vulnerable to the bacteria that may be present on sprouts.

PER SERVING: 252 KCALS | 19.1G FAT | 2G SAT FAT | 17.5G CARBS | 9.8G SUGARS | 4G FIBRE | 8.4G PROTEIN | TRACE SALT

RAW PIZZA

Sometimes all you want after a busy week is pizza. Unlike greasy fast-food pizza, this version is much healthier, with a delectable nutty base and a mouthwatering spinach spreading sauce.

MAKES: 2 X 20-CM/8-INCH PIZZAS TO SERVE 4
PREP: 30 MINS, PLUS DEHYDRATING AND MARINATING

PIZZA BASE

50 g/1³/₄ oz raw walnuts
50 g/1³/₄ oz sunflower seeds
40 g/1¹/₂ oz pumpkin seeds
125 g/4¹/₂ oz hulled hemp seeds
30 g/1 oz milled flaxseed
90 g/3¹/₄ oz buckwheat flour
¹/₂ tsp sea salt and ¹/₂ tsp black pepper
1 celery stick, chopped and 1 small onion, chopped
1 tbsp water, plus extra if necessary

SPINACH SPREADING SAUCE

30 g/1 oz small spinach leaves, chopped
30 g/1 oz fresh basil leaves
30 g/1 oz raw pine nuts
2 garlic cloves, crushed
¹/₂ tsp sea salt and 1 tsp black pepper
2 tbsp cold-pressed extra virgin olive oil

TOPPINGS

6 chestnut mushrooms, sliced
¹/₂ red onion, thinly sliced
12 baby spinach leaves
2 tomatoes, sliced
8 cherry tomatoes, halved
pinch black pepper, to serve

MARINADE

2 tbsp cold-pressed extra virgin olive oil
¹/₂ tbsp raw apple cider vinegar
2 tsp raw coconut aminos
¹/₂ tsp black pepper

1. You will need a dehydrator for this recipe. If you don't have a dehydrator, many electric cookers will dehydrate food on a low enough heat (the dehydrate high setting is 60°C/140°F; the dehydrate low setting is 45°C/115°F). This may be the defrost setting or slightly higher, or a designated dehydrate setting. Check you have the correct temperature with an oven thermometer before dehydrating in a standard cooker.

2. To make the pizza base, pulse the walnuts, sunflower seeds and pumpkin seeds in a food processor for a few seconds until coarsely ground. Tip them into a mixing bowl with the hemp seeds, flaxseed, buckwheat flour, salt and pepper, and stir.

3. Add the celery and onion to the processor and pulse to a purée, then spoon into the mixing bowl. Add the tablespoon of water and mix everything together, adding a little more water and mixing again until you have a fairly dry dough.

4. Shape the dough into 2 x 20-cm/8-inch rounds on non-stick dehydrator sheets. (If using the oven, use a non-stick oven tray.) Dehydrate for 3 hours on low (45°C/115°F), then turn the bases over and dehydrate for a further 3 hours on low, or until lightly crisped and firm.

5. Meanwhile, start preparing the toppings. Put the mushrooms and onion in a shallow non-metallic dish. Mix the marinade ingredients together and pour into the dish, making sure all the vegetables are coated. Cover and leave for 2 hours, to soften and absorb the flavours.

6. To make the spinach spreading sauce, put all the ingredients in a mortar and pound with a pestle. For a smoother spread, you can process the ingredients in a food processor.

7. Spread half the sauce over each pizza base and divide the topping ingredients between each one. Drizzle a little marinade over the pizzas and grind over black pepper to serve.

PER SERVING: 670 KCALS | 50G FAT | 5.5G SAT FAT | 36.1G CARBS | 5.6G SUGARS | 11.8G FIBRE | 25.6G PROTEIN | 1.6G SALT

FALAFEL WITH RAW HUMMUS

Falafel is a popular Middle Eastern dish that's usually deep-fried. This healthy, but just as tasty, raw version is made from sprouted chickpeas and sweet potato, and is served with homemade hummus.

SERVES: 4

PREP: 20 MINS, PLUS SPROUTING AND DEHYDRATING

200 g/7 oz chickpeas suitable for sprouting
175 g/6 oz sweet potato, peeled and roughly chopped
1 tbsp milled flaxseed
1 tbsp raw light tahini
1 tsp ground cumin seeds
1 small medium-hot red chilli, deseeded
2 tsp peeled and chopped fresh ginger
2 tsp raw coconut aminos
1 tbsp chopped fresh parsley
1 tbsp chopped fresh coriander leaves
2 tbsp sesame seeds
sea salt (optional)
black pepper (optional)

RAW HUMMUS

175 g/6 oz courgettes, peeled and roughly chopped
1 tbsp raw light tahini
juice of ½ lemon
2 garlic cloves, crushed
½ tsp ground cumin seeds
¼ tsp sea salt

SALAD

1 small carrot, peeled and sliced
½ red pepper, deseeded and sliced
12 Little Gem lettuce leaves
8 radishes, sliced
4 tsp cold-pressed extra virgin olive oil

1. You will need a dehydrator for this recipe. If you don't have one, many electric cookers will dehydrate food on a low enough heat (the dehydrate high setting is 60°C/140°F; the dehydrate low setting is 45°C/115°F). This may be the defrost setting or slightly higher, or a designated dehydrate setting. Check you have the correct temperature with an oven thermometer before dehydrating in a standard cooker.

2. Start sprouting the chickpeas 3–5 days before you start. Place the chickpeas in a jar and cover with tepid water. Keep in a warm, dark room. Soak for 24 hours, then drain and rinse, and drain again. Rinse and drain twice a day for 3–5 days. When the sprouts are about 8 mm/³/₈ inch long, they are ready.

3. Process the chickpeas and sweet potato in a food processor until you have a fairly smooth but lightly textured mix.

4. Add the flaxseed, tahini, cumin seeds, chilli, ginger and coconut aminos to the processor and blend to combine. Transfer the mixture to a bowl and stir in the parsley and coriander. Season to taste with salt and pepper, if using.

5. Mould the mixture into 20 small balls and roll them in the sesame seeds. Transfer to a non-stick dehydrator sheet on a dehydrator tray. (If using the oven, use a non-stick oven tray.) Dehydrate on low (45°C/115°F) for 6 hours, then turn them over and dehydrate on low for a further 2 hours.

6. To make the salad, mix the vegetables together in a serving bowl and drizzle with the olive oil.

7. To make the hummus, put all the ingredients in a clean processor and blend until you have a fairly smooth mix. Serve the falafels alongside the dip and the salad.

> Note: sprouted chickpeas should be avoided by children younger than five, older adults, pregnant women and those with weakened immune systems.

PER SERVING: 381 KCALS | 14.9G FAT | 1.9G SAT FAT | 51G CARBS | 10.5G SUGARS | 11.3G FIBRE | 14.7G PROTEIN | 0.5G SALT

SPAGHETTI WITH GARLIC CREAM SAUCE AND BABY TOMATOES

It's so easy to make raw spaghetti if you own a spiralizer – this carb-free version creates strands of pasta from courgette and is topped with a velvety garlic sauce.

SERVES: 2
PREP: 20 MINS, PLUS SOAKING

2 courgettes, spiralized
1 tbsp cold-pressed extra virgin olive oil
½ tsp sea salt

GARLIC CREAM SAUCE
100 g/3½ oz raw skinned almonds, soaked in water for 2 hours, drained and rinsed
30 ml/2 tbsp raw almond milk
1 large garlic clove, chopped
1 spring onion, chopped
2 tsp raw apple cider vinegar
½ tsp sea salt

TO SERVE
6 sun-dried tomato pieces
10 baby plum tomatoes, halved
1 spring onion, chopped
2 fresh basil sprigs, leaves separated

1. To make the garlic cream sauce, pulse the soaked almonds in a food processor until they are ground. Add the almond milk, garlic, spring onion, vinegar and salt, and blend until you have a thick, creamy paste. Transfer to a bowl.

2. Toss the courgette spirals in the olive oil and salt. Divide the spirals between two serving bowls.

3. Spoon the creamy sauce into the centre of each bowl, then top with the sun-dried tomatoes, plum tomatoes, spring onions and basil leaves. Serve immediately.

SPAGHETTI OPTIONS
Try different vegetables for your 'spaghetti' as the seasons pass – Italian tromba is lovely in summer and butternut squash is great in winter.

PER SERVING: 428 KCALS | 35.2G FAT | 3.1G SAT FAT | 21.4G CARBS | 9.9G SUGARS | 8.4G FIBRE | 14.7G PROTEIN | 1.5G SALT

GADO GADO
SALAD

For a fresh and nutritious main meal, simply toss raw cauliflower and broccoli with crunchy beansprouts and cucumber and coat them with a delicious raw dressing.

SERVES: 4
PREP: 10–15 MINS

250 g/9 oz cauliflower, cored and cut into small florets
115 g /4 oz broccoli, destalked and cut into small florets
115 g/4 oz Savoy cabbage, shredded
150 g/5 ½ oz ready-to-eat beansprouts
300 g/10 ½ oz cucumber, peeled, halved lenthways, deseeded and thickly sliced
1 red pepper, halved, deseeded and finely chopped

DRESSING
2 tbsp groundnut oil
85 g/3 oz unsalted peanuts, finely chopped
2 garlic cloves, minced
2 tbsp soy sauce
juice of 2 limes
½ red chilli, deseeded and minced

1. Put the cauliflower, broccoli, cabbage, beansprouts, cucumber and red pepper in a salad bowl and toss gently together.

2. To make the dressing, warm 1 tablespoon of the oil in a pan over a low heat (you can warm raw food below a temperature of 40°C/104°F). Add the peanuts and garlic and warm for 2—3 minutes and then remove from the heat and stir in the soy sauce, lime juice, chilli and remaining oil, then leave at room temperature for a couple of hours.

3. When ready to eat, stir the dressing thoroughly, spoon it over the salad and toss them gently together. Spoon into four bowls, then serve immediately.

MUNG BEANSPROUTS
Mung beansprouts, widely available in supermarkets all year round, are a good addition to this recipe. Low in calories, they also have fibre, B vitamins, and vitamins C and K.

PER SERVING: 259 KCALS | 17.8G FAT | 2.6G SAT FAT | 19.9G CARBS | 7.7G SUGARS | 6.6G FIBRE | 10.2G PROTEIN | 0.1G SALT

DESSERTS AND SWEET TREATS

PEACH AND ORANGE GRANITA

A fruity Italian granita makes a quick and refreshingly light dessert. By using fruit pulp instead of just juice, you also get lots of fibre and vitamin C.

SERVES: 4
PREP: 10 MINS, PLUS FREEZING

juice of 2 large oranges
4 peaches, stoned and peeled
juice of 1 lime
3 tbsp raw agave nectar
seeds from ½ vanilla pod
1 orange, cut into slices, to decorate
4 fresh mint leaves, to decorate

1. Put the orange juice, peaches, lime juice, agave nectar and vanilla seeds in a blender and blend until smooth, or until a few small peach pieces are left.

2. Pour the mixture into a shallow, lidded, freezable container and freeze for 2 hours.

3. Stir the mixture with a fork, bringing the frozen edges into the centre. Replace the lid and freeze for another 2 hours.

4. Stir again and freeze for another hour, or until nearly frozen in the centre. Stir again before dividing the granita between four glasses. Serve decorated with the orange slices and mint leaves.

FRUIT FAVOURITES
You can try the same recipe using 1 large ripe mango, 2 papayas or 4 nectarines instead of the peach.

PER SERVING: 142 KCALS | 0.5G FAT | TRACE SAT FAT | 34.9G CARBS | 30.6G SUGARS | 3.2G FIBRE | 2G PROTEIN | TRACE SALT

MIXED FRUIT
SOUP BOWL

This summery cold fruit soup is perfect for a hot day, and is rich in antioxidants due to its lovely bright colours. Papaya is also a rich source of proteolytic enzymes, mainly papain, which greatly aid the digestive process.

SERVES: 4
PREP: 15 MINS, PLUS CHILLING

2 papaya, peeled, deseeded and chopped
300 g/10½ oz strawberries, hulled
1 honeydew melon, deseeded, peeled and chopped
15 g/½ oz fresh mint leaves
1 tbsp stem ginger syrup
1 knob of stem ginger
100 g/3½ oz blueberries

1. Reserving 1 tablespoon of the chopped papaya, place the remainder in a food processor with 280 g/10 oz of the strawberries and process to a smooth purée.

2. Pour into a jug and chill in the refrigerator for 10 minutes.

3. Place all but 1 tablespoon of the chopped melon in the food processor with half the mint leaves, the ginger syrup and stem ginger. Process to a smooth purée. Pour into a jug and chill in the refrigerator for 10 minutes.

4. When you are ready to serve, divide each soup between four bowls, then use a knife to swirl them together. Drop a couple of ice cubes into each bowl.

5. Dice the reserved fruits and sprinkle over the soup, together with the blueberries and the remaining mint leaves.

FRUITS OF CHANGE
When possible, use fruits that are in season. This is also delicious made with raspberries instead of strawberries, and is just as healthy.

PER SERVING: 173 KCALS | 0.9G FAT | 0.2G SAT FAT | 43.1G CARBS | 34.4G SUGARS | 5.7G FIBRE | 2.2G PROTEIN | 0.1G SALT

CACAO, CHILLI AND AVOCADO MOUSSE WITH CINNAMON BERRIES

Here's an unusual dessert that you definitely don't have to feel guilty for enjoying – it is full of healthy ingredients and sweetened with agave nectar rather than sugar.

SERVES: 4

PREP: 4 HRS 15 MINS

2 ripe avocados, halved and stoned
60 g/2¼ oz cacao powder
4 tbsp agave nectar
seeds from ½ vanilla pod
½ tsp chilli powder
50 ml/2 fl oz canned full–fat coconut milk
40 g/1½ oz wild strawberries, or small strawberries
40 g/1½ oz fresh raspberries
½ tsp ground cinnamon

1. Scoop the avocado flesh into a large bowl and mash lightly with fork. Stir in the cacao powder, agave nectar, vanilla seeds and chilli powder. Blend thoroughly with a hand blender until the mixture is thick and smooth. Stir in the coconut milk and blend again.

2. Spoon the avocado mixture into ramekins or small, stemmed glasses. Cover with clingfilm and chill for at least 4 hours.

3. Decorate the avocado mousses evenly with the berries and sprinkle the cinnamon over each dish. Serve immediately.

CACAO RICHNESS
Cacao is rich in antioxidants including flavonoids and catechins – its antioxidant level is higher even than green and black tea, and cacao is also packed with fibre.

PER SERVING: 249 KCALS | 15.8G FAT | 5.1G SAT FAT | 32.9G CARBS | 17G SUGARS | 11.7G FIBRE | 4.9G PROTEIN | TRACE SALT

LAYERED APPLE PIE

This raw apple pie is a delicious, contemporary twist on a beloved classic. With its magical layers of apple, dates and spices, it tastes even better than the original.

SERVES: 8
PREP: 20 MINS, PLUS SOAKING, FREEZING AND CHILLING

175 g/6 oz raw walnuts
100 g/3½ oz Medjool dates, stoned
2 tbsp melted cold-pressed, extra virgin coconut oil
200 g/7 oz Medjool dates, stoned, soaked in water for 4 hours, drained and rinsed
1 small banana, peeled and roughly chopped
1 apple, peeled, cored and roughly chopped
1 tsp ground cinnamon
½ tsp ground nutmeg
1 tsp seeds from 1 vanilla pod
½ tsp sea salt
juice of ½ lemon
5 dessert apples, cored
60 g/2¼ oz sultanas
½ tsp ground cinnamon, for dusting

1. Line a 20-cm/8-inch x 6-cm/2½-inch round tin with non-stick baking paper. Set aside.

2. To make the pie crust, pulse the walnuts in a processor for a few seconds, then add the dates and process again until you have a fine, sticky mix. Add the coconut oil and blend again.

3. Spoon the mixture into the prepared tin. Press down thoroughly and evenly, and put in the freezer to set for 1½–2 hours.

4. To make the filling, put the soaked dates, banana and apple in a clean processor with the cinnamon, nutmeg, vanilla seeds and salt. Pulse to thoroughly combine, then spoon into a mixing bowl.

5. Stir the lemon juice into a bowl of cold water. Using a mandolin or sharp knife, thinly slice the dessert apples, adding them to the water bowl as you go (the acid from the lemon stops them turning brown).

6. Spoon a thin layer of the filling onto the chilled pie crust and top with a few of the sultanas and a layer of sliced apples. Push the apple slices down well. Repeat until you have used all the filling, sliced apples and sultanas, then dust the top of the pie with the cinnamon. Chill in the fridge for an hour before serving.

VARIATION
You can make a similar pie using firm dessert pears instead of apples.

PER SERVING: 375 KCALS | 18.4G FAT | 4.4G SAT FAT | 56.2G CARBS | 43.2G SUGARS | 7.6G FIBRE | 4.8G PROTEIN | TRACE SALT

RAW BANANA, PINEAPPLE AND PEANUT PIE

Here's a raw version of tempting banoffee pie – made even better with the addition of pineapple and peanut butter! It's rich and smooth, with a gorgeous mixed nut crust.

SERVES: 8
PREP: 15 MINS, PLUS SOAKING AND FREEZING

PIE CRUST
125 g/4½ oz raw hazelnuts
125 g/4½ oz raw Brazil nuts
85 g/3 oz raw pecan nuts
4 Medjool dates, stoned and chopped
1½ tbsp maple syrup
2 tbsp melted cold-pressed extra virgin coconut oil
1 tbsp water

FILLING
4 ripe bananas, chopped
4 tbsp raw peanut butter
3 slices ripe pineapple, chopped
1½ tbsp raw creamed coconut, melted
½ tsp sea salt

TOPPING
1 banana, sliced and soaked in
50 ml/2 fl oz pineapple juice for 30 minutes
2 thin slices pineapple, chopped, to decorate
8 raw pecan nut halves, to decorate

1. Line a 20-cm/8-inch x 6-cm/2½-inch round pan with non-stick baking paper. Set aside.

2. To make the pie crust, put all the nuts in a food processor and pulse for a few seconds. Add the dates, maple syrup, coconut oil and water. Process until you have a crumbly, fairly fine mixture.

3. Press the nut mixture evenly and firmly into the prepared pan. Chill in the freezer for 2 hours.

4. Meanwhile, make the filling. Put all the ingredients in a food processor and process until the mixture is thoroughly blended. Spoon the filling onto the frozen crust and smooth the top. Freeze again for an hour, or until the filling is firm.

5. To make the topping, arrange the soaked banana slices over the pie with the pineapple pieces and pecan nut halves. Keep the pie in the fridge until ready to serve.

> ### GRATE THE GARNISH
> Grate some raw cacao nibs over the top of the pie just before serving.

PER SERVING: 501 KCALS | 37.4G FAT | 9.6G SAT FAT | 42.1G CARBS | 25.8G SUGARS | 7.6G FIBRE | 8.7G PROTEIN | 0.4G SALT

CHOCOLATE AVOCADO LIME PIE

*With its nutty crust, luscious avocado filling and chocolate topping,
this pie is true decadence – but because it's packed with vital nutrients,
healthy fats and fibre, it's actually good for you!*

SERVES: 8
PREP: 30 MINS, PLUS SOAKING AND CHILLING

5 Medjool dates, stoned and roughly chopped
70 g/2½ oz raw macadamia nuts
70 g/2½ oz raw pecan nuts
100 g/3½ oz raw Brazil nuts
1 tbsp raw agave nectar
1 tbsp melted cold-pressed extra virgin coconut oil

AVOCADO FILLING

175 g/6 oz raw cashew nuts, soaked in water for 4 hours, drained and rinsed
150 g/5½ oz fresh coconut flesh
50 g/1¾ oz raw creamed coconut, melted
2 ripe avocados, peeled, stoned and roughly chopped
juice of 2 limes
1 tbsp melted cold-pressed extra virgin coconut oil
4 tbsp raw agave nectar

CHOCOLATE TOPPING

70 g/2½ oz raw cashew nuts
2 tbsp raw cacao powder
1 tbsp melted cold-pressed extra virgin coconut oil
4 tbsp raw creamed coconut, melted
4 tbsp raw agave nectar
1 tbsp water
30 g/1 oz fresh coconut flesh, shaved, to decorate

1. Line a 20-cm/8-inch baking tin with non-stick baking paper and set aside.

2. Put the dates in a small bowl and soak for 10 minutes in enough warm water to cover. Drain and reserve the soaking water.

3. To make the pie crust, pulse the macadamia nuts, pecan nuts and Brazil nuts in a food processor for 10 seconds, then add the soaked dates and pulse again until everything is finely chopped. Add the agave nectar, soaking water and coconut oil, and pulse again.

4. Press the mixture into the prepared tin and chill in the fridge for 2 hours, until firm.

5. To make the avocado filling, pulse the soaked cashew nuts in a clean processor until you have a creamy purée. Transfer to a mixing bowl. Process the coconut flesh to a paste, adding a little of the creamed coconut as necessary. Add the coconut to the mixing bowl.

6. Add the avocados to the processor with the lime juice, and pulse to a purée. Transfer to the mixing bowl. Stir in the rest of the creamed coconut, the coconut oil and the agave nectar. Combine everything thoroughly.

7. Spread the filling over the firm crust and smooth the top. Chill in the fridge for another 2 hours.

8. Meanwhile, make the chocolate topping. Cream the cashew nuts as before and transfer to a small mixing bowl. Stir in the rest of the ingredients, reserving the coconut shavings for decoration.

9. When the filling is cool and firm, spread or pipe the topping over the pie. Decorate with the coconut shavings and chill until ready to serve.

PER SERVING: 784 KCALS | 63.8G FAT | 27.2G SAT FAT | 52.9G CARBS | 32.3G SUGARS | 11.3G FIBRE | 12G PROTEIN | TRACE SALT

CREAMY FIG SQUARES

These elegant fig squares are impressive to look at but easy to make! They're made with a high-fibre selection of fruit and nuts, then topped with a sweet almond cream.

MAKES: 9 SQUARES
PREP: 20 MINS, PLUS SOAKING AND FREEZING

70 g/2½ oz moist sun-dried figs
70 g/2½ oz Medjool dates, stoned
50 g/1¾ oz raw walnuts
60 g/2¼ oz raw Brazil nuts
2 tbsp milled flaxseed
½ tbsp melted cold-pressed extra virgin coconut oil

TOPPING
60 g/2¼ oz raw almonds, soaked in water for 4 hours, drained and rinsed
125 ml/4 fl oz raw almond milk
2 tbsp raw coconut flour
1½ tbsp raw agave nectar
1 tsp seeds from 1 vanilla pod
1 tbsp melted cold-pressed extra virgin coconut oil
5 fresh figs
2 fresh figs, sliced, to decorate

1. Line an 18-cm/7-inch tin with non-stick baking paper and set aside.

2. Put the sun-dried figs, dates, nuts, flaxseed and coconut oil in a food processor and pulse until you have a crumbly, sticky mixture. Press into the prepared tin and freeze for 1–2 hours, until firm.

3. To make the topping, rub the skins off the soaked almonds – they should come away easily – and put them in a clean processor, reserving 5 for decoration. Pulse until you have a thick, creamy purée, then add the almond milk, coconut flour, agave nectar, vanilla seeds and coconut oil. Blend again.

4. Scoop the flesh out of the 5 fresh figs and mash them with a fork in a small bowl. Stir this into the topping mixture.

5. Smooth the topping over the frozen mixture and freeze again for 1–2 hours. When firm, cut into squares and top each square with a slice of fresh fig. Chop the 5 reserved almonds and put a little on each fig slice. Serve the squares chilled.

PARTY SNACKS
Cut each square into four small bites and serve them as snacks at a dinner party.

PER SQUARE: 242 KCALS | 16.1G FAT | 4G SAT FAT | 23.9G CARBS | 17.9G SUGARS | 5G FIBRE | 4.9G PROTEIN | TRACE SALT

ALMOND AND BERRY PICK-ME-UP BARS

If you're feeling hungry between meals or your energy's dipped, one of these chocolate-and coconut-infused, nutrient-packed treats will pick you right up.

MAKES: 10 BARS
PREP: 15 MINS, PLUS SOAKING AND DEHYDRATING

70 g/2½ oz pumpkin seeds
60 g/2¼ oz sunflower seeds
125 g/4½ oz raw almonds, soaked in water for 4 hours, drained and rinsed
30 g/1 oz milled flaxseed
4 tbsp raw agave nectar
1½ tsp ground cinnamon
40 g/1½ oz goji berries, soaked in water for 30 minutes, drained and rinsed
50 g/1¾ oz cacao nibs
2 tbsp chopped goldenberries
1 tbsp sesame seeds
1½ tbsp buckwheat flour
1½ tbsp raw creamed coconut

CHOCOLATE TOPPING

70 g/2½ oz raw cashew nuts, soaked in water for 4 hours, drained and rinsed
2 tbsp raw cacao powder
2 tbsp melted cold-pressed extra virgin coconut oil
2 tbsp raw creamed coconut, melted
4 tbsp raw honey

1. You will need a dehydrator for this recipe. If you don't have a dehydrator, many electric cookers will dehydrate food on a low enough heat (the dehydrate high setting is 60°C/140°F; the dehydrate low setting is 45°C/115°F). This may be the defrost setting or slightly higher, or a designated dehydrate setting. Check you have the correct temperature with an oven thermometer before dehydrating in a standard cooker.

2. Soak two thirds of the pumpkin and sunflower seeds in water for 4 hours. Drain and rinse.

3. Line a 20-cm/8-inch shallow container with non-stick baking paper. (If using the oven, line an oven tray with parchment paper.) Set aside.

4. Grind the soaked almonds and seeds in a food processor. Add the flaxseed, agave nectar and cinnamon to the processor and pulse until well combined. Tip the mixture into a mixing bowl.

5. Add the rest of the seeds to the bowl with the soaked goji berries, cacao nibs, goldenberries, sesame seeds, buckwheat flour and creamed coconut. Stir well.

6. Press the mixture into the prepared container and dehydrate on high (60°C/140°F) for an hour, then on low (45°C/115°F) for 3 hours.

7. Remove the mixture from the tin and cut into 10 bars. Line a dehydrator tray with a non-stick dehydrator sheet. (If using the oven, use a parchment-lined oven tray.) Transfer the bars to the sheet and dehydrate again on low, until they are dry on the outside but still a little soft on the inside.

8. Meanwhile, make the topping. Pulse the soaked cashew nuts in a clean processor until smooth and creamy. Spoon into a mixing bowl, add the rest of the ingredients and mix well with a fork.

9. When the bars are completely cool, coat them with the chocolate topping and chill in the fridge until set.

PER BAR: 363 KCALS | 25.6G FAT | 8.4G SAT FAT | 30.9G CARBS | 18.3G SUGARS | 7.4G FIBRE | 10.1G PROTEIN | TRACE SALT

CASHEW COOKIES

These energy-boosting, nut-packed cookies couldn't be any easier to make. Soft-centred and light, but without all the refined sugar, you'll be making them for kids and adults alike.

MAKES: 16 COOKIES
PREP: 10 MINS, PLUS SOAKING AND DEHYDRATING

100 g/3½ oz raw cashew nuts, soaked in water for 4 hours, drained and rinsed
100 g/3½ oz raw coconut flour, plus 1 tbsp for dusting
50 ml/2 fl oz raw coconut milk
2 tbsp raw agave nectar
½ tsp sea salt
½ tsp seeds from 1 vanilla pod

1. You will need a dehydrator for this recipe. If you don't have a dehydrator, many electric cookers will dehydrate food on a low enough heat (the dehydrate high setting is 60°C/140°F; the dehydrate low setting is 45°C/115°F). This may be the defrost setting or slightly higher, or a designated dehydrate setting. Check you have the correct temperature with an oven thermometer before dehydrating in a standard cooker.

2. Pulse the soaked cashew nuts in a food processor until you have a smooth nut butter.

3. Sieve the coconut flour into a mixing bowl and stir in the cashew butter and the remaining ingredients. Mix well with a fork until you have a soft dough.

4. Cover the dough and chill in the fridge for 2 hours. Meanwhile, line a dehydrator tray with a non–stick dehydrator sheet and set aside. (If using the oven, line an oven tray with parchment paper.)

5. Roll the chilled dough into 16 small balls using your hands. Place them on the prepared sheet and flatten a little. (If using the oven, add the balls to your oven tray lined with parchment paper.) Using a fork, rake a pattern over the surface of each cookie. Dust with a sieved tablespoon of coconut flour.

6. Dehydrate the cookies on low (45°C/115°F) for approximately 10 hours, or until they are lightly crisp on the outside but still a little soft in the centre. Store in the fridge.

FLOUR POWER
Try using almond flour and almond butter for a different flavour.

PER COOKIE: 68 KCALS | 4G FAT | 1.6G SAT FAT | 4.6G CARBS | 2.9G SUGARS | 3.6G FIBRE | 2.4G PROTEIN | 0.2G SALT

NO-BAKE CARROT CAKE

Tender shavings of carrot are a perfect addition to any cake or dessert, but they taste particularly sweet and juicy in a raw dessert.

SERVES: 8
PREP: 20 MINS, PLUS SOAKING AND CHILLING

2 large carrots, roughly chopped (about 250 g/9 oz prepared carrot)
55 g/2 oz fresh coconut flesh, roughly chopped
100 g/3½ oz sun-dried organic apricots
85 g/3 oz raw walnuts
200 g/7 oz Medjool dates, stoned
70 g/2½ oz buckwheat flour
50 g/1¾ oz raw coconut flour
1 tsp ground cinnamon
½ tsp sea salt
2 tbsp orange juice
8 raw walnut halves, to decorate

RAW CASHEW CREAM
200 g/7 oz raw cashew nuts, soaked in water for 4 hours, drained and rinsed
2 tbsp orange juice
2½ tbsp melted cold-pressed extra virgin coconut oil
2 tbsp maple syrup

1. Line an 18-cm/7-inch round cake tin with non-stick baking paper and set aside.

2. To make the cashew cream, blend the soaked nuts with half the orange juice in a food processor until creamy, then add the remaining ingredients and process until smooth. Transfer the cream to a bowl and keep in the fridge

3. For the cake, pulse the carrots and coconut in a food processor for a few seconds, then add the apricots, half the walnuts and half the dates. Process until everything is finely chopped.

4. Transfer the cake mixture to a large mixing bowl. Roughly chop the remaining walnuts and dates, and add to the bowl. In a separate bowl, combine the flours, cinnamon and salt, then tip into the cake mixture and combine thoroughly until all the flour is incorporated. Add the orange juice and stir well.

5. Spoon half the cake mixture evenly into the prepared tin. Top with half the cashew cream and smooth the top. Freeze for 2 hours.

6. Remove the cake from the freezer and spoon the rest of the cake mixture over the cream. Top with the remaining cream. Freeze for a further hour, then decorate with the walnut halves.

CREATE, THEN DECORATE
Decorate the finished cake as you like – instead of the walnuts, you could try sun-dried fruit pieces, such as apricots or mangoes.

PER SERVING: 460 KCALS | 26.9G FAT | 9.2G SAT FAT | 50.9G CARBS | 31.2G SUGARS | 9.8G FIBRE | 10.2G PROTEIN | 0.4G SALT

ALMOND AND PISTACHIO BROWNIES

These brownies taste incredibly indulgent, but are in fact low in sugar and full of healthy ingredients. As an added bonus, they provide antioxidants, vitamin E, iron, fibre and monounsaturated fats.

MAKES: 16 BROWNIES
PREP: 10 MINS, PLUS CHILLING

125 g/4½ oz raw almonds
100 g/3½ oz raw pistachio nuts
2 tbsp raw cacao powder
300 g/10½ oz Medjool dates, stoned
1 tsp seeds from 1 vanilla pod
1 tsp sea salt
50 g/1¾ oz raw cacao nibs, chopped

TOPPING

3 tbsp raw cacao powder
4 tbsp raw honey
2 tbsp melted cold-pressed extra virgin coconut oil
½ tsp seeds from 1 vanilla pod
50 ml/2 fl oz raw almond milk
1 tbsp chopped raw pistachio nuts, to decorate

1. Line a 20-cm/8-inch square tin with non-stick baking paper and set aside.

2. Reserve 30 g/1 oz almonds and 20g/¾ oz pistachio nuts. Pulse the remaining nuts in a food processor until you have fairly fine crumbs. Add the cacao powder, dates, vanilla seeds and salt, and pulse again to form a thick mixture.

3. Transfer the brownie mixture to a bowl and stir in the reserved nuts and the cacao nibs. Press it evenly into the prepared tin.

4. To make the topping, blend the cacao powder, honey, coconut oil and vanilla seeds in a blender with enough of the almond milk to make a fairly thick sauce. Pour this over the brownie mixture and sprinkle over the pistachio nuts. Chill in the fridge for an hour, or until the topping is set.

5. Cut the brownie into 16 squares and store in the fridge.

SWAP THE NUTS
For another nutty and equally delicious brownie, replace the almonds and pistachio nuts with walnuts and pecan nuts.

PER BROWNIE: 181 KCALS | 9.7G FAT | 2.6G SAT FAT | 24.9G CARBS | 17.7G SUGARS | 4.7G FIBRE | 4.1G PROTEIN | 0.4G SALT

PASTEL MELTS

Serve these pretty little treats as part of a buffet or to impress your guests at the end of a dinner party. They come in three different flavours and melt in the mouth.

MAKES: 15 MELTS
PREP: 15 MINS, PLUS CHILLING

LEMON MELTS
40 g/1½ oz ground almonds
15 g/½ oz raw coconut flour
1⅓ tbsp lemon juice
½ tbsp raw agave nectar
1 tbsp melted cold-pressed extra virgin coconut oil
pinch sea salt
2 tbsp grated fresh coconut

PISTACHIO MELTS
30 g/1 oz raw pistachio nuts
20 g/¾ oz ground almonds
15 g/½ oz raw coconut flour
½ tbsp raw agave nectar
1½ tbsp melted cold-pressed extra virgin coconut oil
½ tsp seeds from 1 vanilla pod
pinch sea salt

MANGO MELTS
40 g/1½ oz ground almonds
15 g/½ oz raw coconut flour, plus 1 tbsp for dusting
2 tbsp puréed fresh mango
½ tbsp raw agave nectar
½ tbsp melted cold-pressed extra virgin coconut oil
½ tsp seeds from 1 vanilla pod
pinch sea salt

1. To make the lemon melts, combine all the ingredients, except the grated coconut, in a small mixing bowl. Using your hands, form the mixture into 5 balls and roll them in the coconut. Move to a plate and chill in the fridge for 30 minutes.

2. To make the pistachio melts, grind the nuts in a processor. Set aside 10 g/¼ nuts and add the rest to a small mixing bowl with the remaining ingredients. Mix thoroughly, then form the mixture into 5 balls and roll them in the remaining nuts. Move to a plate and chill in the fridge for 30 minutes.

3. To make the mango melts, combine all the ingredients, except 1 tbsp coconut flour, in a small mixing bowl, then form the mixture into 5 balls. Sieve the remaining coconut flour over them. Move to a plate and chill in the fridge for 30 minutes.

4. Take the melts out of the fridge 5 minutes before serving.

PAPAYA MELT
You can also make papaya melts by mixing 40 g/ 1½ oz ground almonds, 2 tablespoons of ripe papaya flesh, half a tablespoon of melted coconut oil and half a teaspoon of vanilla pod seeds. Roll the mixture into 5 balls, decorate with 2 tablespoons of grated fresh coconut and chill for 30 minutes.

PER LEMON MELT: 95 KCALS | 8G FAT | 3.6G SAT FAT | 3.8G CARBS | 2.4G SUGARS | 2.5G FIBRE | 2.3G PROTEIN | 0.3G SALT
PER PISTACHIO MELT: 108 KCALS | 9.3G FAT | 4.4G SAT FAT | 4.2G CARBS | 2.4G SUGARS | 2.5G FIBRE | 2.6G PROTEIN | 0.3G SALT
PER MANGO MELT: 82 KCALS | 6.1G FAT | 1.9G SAT FAT | 4.3G CARBS | 3G SUGARS | 2.9G FIBRE | 2.5G PROTEIN | 0.3G SALT

INDEX